The Complete Guitar Player

by Russ Shipton.

Books 1,2,3 and 4

Omnibus Edition

Amsco Publications
New York/London/Sydney

Contents

Contents

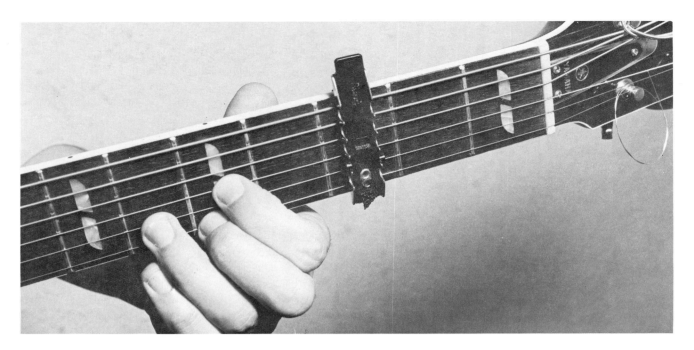

About the Capo

Most folk guitarists use this important device. The capo shortens the guitar strings and increases their pitch by the same amount. It can be placed on any fret (just behind the fret wire).

If the pitch of a song doesn't suit your vocal range, the capo can be put somewhere on the neck of the guitar. The position of the capo can be changed until the melody suits your voice. The same chord shapes can be played as before, but singing will be easier.

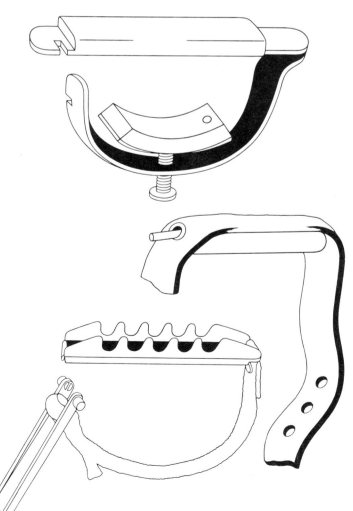

Using The Capo

To be effective, the capo must press all the strings down firmly. The first capo uses a screw to make it tight. The second is made of strong elastic that is stretched around the guitar neck until a hole fits onto the pin. The third type is made of a strong, synthetic fiber attached to a piece of plastic – this fits into metal teeth. When the piece of plastic is pressed down, the capo is secured. (See the photograph, where this type of capo is shown on the third fret.)

Two people can use different groups of chord shapes and still play together if one of them uses a capo. Try these two possibilities:

1st Player (or group)
Chords **A, D**, and **E** (No capo)
2nd Player (or group)
Chord shapes **D, G**, and **A** (capo on 7th fret)

1st Player (or group)
Chords **D, G**, and **A** (No capo)
2nd Player (or group)
Chord shapes **A, D**, and **E** (capo on 5th fret)

The Complete Guitar Player

by Russ Shipton.

Songs and music in this book
Amazing Grace
Blowin' In The Wind
Catch The Wind
Colours
English Country Garden
The Last Thing On My Mind
Leaving On A Jet Plane
Me And Bobby McGee
Scarborough Fair
The Times They Are A-Changin'

Amsco Publications   New York/London/Sydney/Cologne

Your Guitar

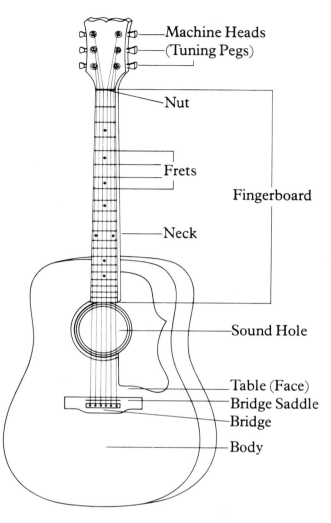

Machine Heads (Tuning Pegs)

Nut

Frets

Fingerboard

Neck

Sound Hole

Table (Face)
Bridge Saddle
Bridge
Body

The Capo.

It would be very useful for you to have a "capo." This device helps to make the level of playing (the pitch of the notes) suit the range of the voice.

Holding Your Guitar

When playing modern guitar styles, this is the sort of position you can use...

The Right Hand For strumming, hold the fingers together. For picking styles, put the wrist out to the front slightly, and keep the thumb a bit to the left of the fingers, which are held over the three treble strings.

The Left Hand The fingertips press the strings down. The palm of the hand should be kept clear of the neck. The thumb should be behind the 1st and 2nd fingers, midway on the neck for a good grip and free movement.

General The crook of your arm should grip on the "corner" of the body of the guitar. Then your right hand should fall over the rear half of the sound hole.

Both hands should be clear of the guitar, giving the fingers room to move. Try not to have a cramped position. It takes just a couple of weeks to get used to the right position.

Tuning Your Guitar

You must tune your guitar every time you pick it up. Firstly, you will have a better chance of producing nice sounds; and secondly your "ear" or sense of pitch will improve.

The easiest way to tune your guitar is to use the **Guitar Tuning Record** which comes with this book. The note on each string is sounded at correct concert pitch and is held long enough for you to tune it. In addition, there are full instructions on the method of raising or lowering the notes on the strings.

In case, for some reason, you are unable to use the **Guitar Tuning Record,** here is a method which is traditionally used to tune the guitar:

Relative Tuning

Wind the 6th string until it feels and sounds right. Then follow these steps:

Tune your 5th string to your 6th string. Put your finger (left-hand) on the 5th fret of the 6th string and play that note with your right hand thumb. Now play the open 5th string ("open" means with no finger pressing on it). These two notes should be the same. If they are not, wind the 5th string up or down and check again and again till they are the same. Remember: you wind the string **up** if it is too low, **down** if it is too high.

Tune your open 4th string to the 5th string. This time, press the 5th fret of the 5th string and sound the note. It should be the same as that on the open 4th. If it is not, adjust as described above.

Tune your open 3rd string to the 4th string, 5th fret.
Tune your open 2nd string to the 3rd string, 4th fret.
Tune your open 1st string to the 2nd string, 5th fret.

The following diagram shows you the first five frets of the guitar fingerboard:

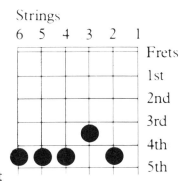

Strings

6 5 4 3 2 1

Frets
1st
2nd
3rd
4th
5th

Your First Chord

Hold your guitar as shown on the previous page, and try to finger an **A** chord. The diagram below is a chord "window" showing the end of the fingerboard (imagine the guitar neck pointing to the sky). Thus the strings are going down the page. The numbers in circles tell you which finger to use. Your index finger is 1, middle 2, ring 3, and little one 4. The picture below shows you how the chord should look. All three fingers are on the same fret so twist your hand to the left slightly. Try to have a slight gap between the neck of the guitar and your hand.

The **A** Chord
Strings

6 5 4 3 2 1

Frets
1st
❶ ❷ ❸
2nd
3rd
4th
5th

Press all three fingers down firmly, with your thumb about midway on the back of the neck, and play each string (start with the bass, 6th string) with your right-hand thumb. Play the strings slowly, one by one, and move your finger or hand to stop any buzzing. Got a clean sound now? Good. Let's have a look at two more chords so you can play your first song . . .

Amazing Grace Warm Up

1 + 2 = 3 Magic Chords

Thousands of songs can be played with just three chords. The two other chords that are usually found with the **A** chord are the **D** and **E** chords...

D

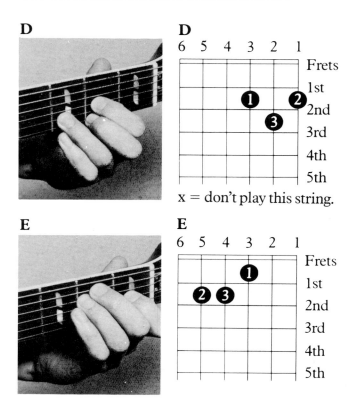

D

6	5	4	3	2	1	
						Frets
						1st
			❶		❷	2nd
				❸		3rd
						4th
						5th

x = don't play this string.

E

E

6	5	4	3	2	1	
						Frets
			❶			1st
❷	❸					2nd
						3rd
						4th
						5th

Put your fingers in the right place and press down firmly. Your thumb should be behind the first and second fingers, midway on the back of the neck. Like you did with the **A** chord, play each string, bass to treble, with your right hand thumb. If you get some buzzing, here are some possible reasons for the trouble:

You're not pressing down on the strings hard enough. This may be due to your nails being too long.

The back of another finger is getting in the way. Or your hand is touching the 1st string. Try to adjust your fingers and hand so the fingertips come down precisely on the proper strings.

Your finger is not close enough to the metal strip in front of it. The further away from the strip you are, the harder you'll have to press to avoid buzzing. With some chords, like the **A**, you can't always get every finger right next to it, but try to get as close as you can.

Your First Strum

Right, can you play all three chords cleanly? Fine, now finger your old favorite, the **A** chord again, and try a strum downwards with your right hand. Holding them together, brush down with the backs of your fingers across all the strings from top to bottom. Not much buzzing? Good. Don't do it too slowly, and extend your fingers as your hand moves downwards. Now try this simple rhythm...

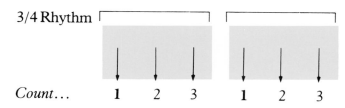

3/4 Rhythm

Count...   1   2   3   1   2   3

Count the beats **1** 2 3, **1** 2 3, **1** 2 3, etc., as shown beneath the arrows (strums). The rhythm is made by making one regular strum heavier than the others. Here it's the first of every three, and the rhythm is called "3/4." The "3" part is what you've got to worry about for the moment, and that's what you're counting beneath the arrows.

Now finger the **D** chord (and then the **E**) and do the same strumming pattern. Take it quite slowly to begin with, and make sure the strums are evenly spaced. Then try to change chords with the left hand **while keeping the rhythm steady with the right.** Once you can do this, have a go at the accompaniment on the next page. Don't try to go fast to begin with. Otherwise you'll have to stop to change chords, and it'll be hard to break the habit.

Amazing Grace Traditional, arranged Russ Shipton

Accompaniment 3/4 Rhythm | = Strum Downwards   **A D E** = Chords

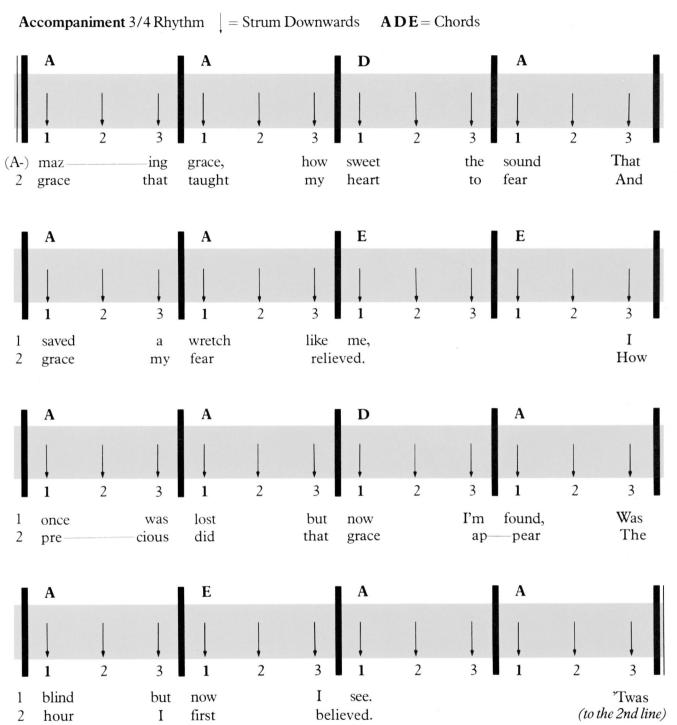

Notes

Bar Lines separate the groups of three strums.
The 1st beat (strum) in each bar is the heavy one.
Length of strums – don't try to hit all the strings on
every strum. Perhaps you can start by hitting five or
six strings on the heavy strum, and three or four
strings on the others. Don't hit the guitar too hard!
Sing "A" of Amazing first, and then begin
strumming on "maz."

Catch The Wind Warm Up

Singing

Most people find singing a little strange at first, but almost everybody is able to pitch their voice correctly to make a reasonable sound. So persevere, even if you feel a little awkward now. I've made the timing of the singing a little easier to follow than the original songs in many cases. When you're in complete control of the playing side of things, time the words as you feel fit. It would help your general progress if you committed the first verse (and chorus where appropriate) to memory.

Upstrokes

Now you've got the simple 3/4 strum pattern mastered, let's complicate things with upstrokes. As your fingers come up for the next strum down, they catch some treble strings on the way. These upstrokes are off the beat and not so "important" as the downstrokes, so they can be hit lightly. Only one or two or three treble strings need be played.

Try this(with an **A** chord):

Down   Up

1   &

Now several in a row(finger a **D** chord this time):

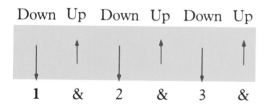

Down Up Down Up Down Up

1   &   2   &   3   &

Chord Changing

We're using the same chords for this song as we did for the last. Can you remember them without looking at the diagrams? The sooner you are able to remember the chords, the quicker you'll progress.

If you're having difficulty changing chords, try to put your first finger down first, and your others just after. Gradually you'll find that you can put them down all together!

Because your left hand won't be very quick at changing for a while, don't go racing away with your right-hand rhythm. Take all accompaniments slowly to begin with, and then you won't have to stop or slow down to get into the next chord position. When you can play the whole song at a slow tempo, the right hand can speed up to a reasonable level.

In "Catch The Wind," the first pattern shown has just one upstroke. Count it **1**, 2 & 3. Each down-stroke is still equally spaced. The other pattern has two upstrokes: **1**& 2& 3. First of all, play every bar with the pattern in the first bar. Then try playing the song with the second pattern. Finally try the accompaniment as shown, with alternating patterns. It's a lot to remember, especially while singing, but it's worth it!

Catch The Wind Donovan

Accompaniment 3/4 Rhythm   ↓↑ = Strum Down and Up

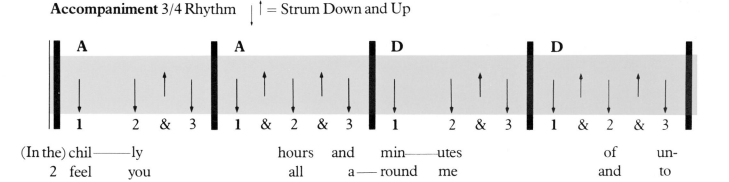

(In the) chil——ly
2 feel   you   hours   and   min——utes   of   un-
                                              all   a——round   me   and   to

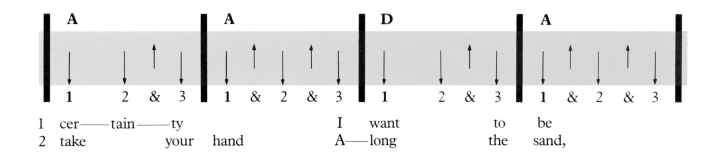

1 cer——tain——ty   I   want   to   be
2 take   your   hand   A——long   the   sand,

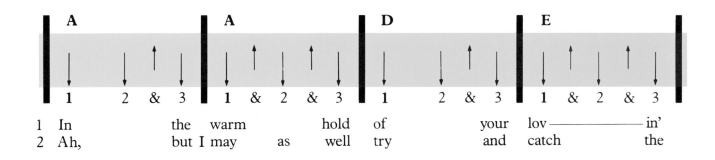

1 In   the   warm   hold   of   your   lov——————in'
2 Ah,   but I may   as   well   try   and   catch   the

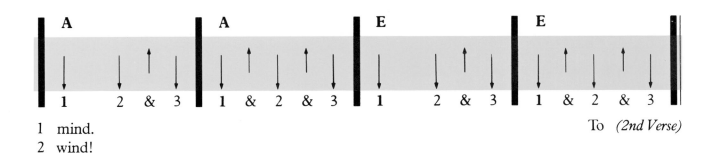

1 mind.   To *(2nd Verse)*
2 wind!

Notes
Play slowly at first. When you can remember the
sequence, try singing the top lines of words. The
second half of the verse has the same chord
sequence. Now try "Amazing Grace" with some
upstrokes.

Leaving On A Jet Plane Warm Up

What's a Chord?

Because we're sticking to the same three chords for this and the next song, you'll get to know them perfectly. But what are chords? Well, they consist of several notes that sound pretty good when played together.

Count the notes in each chord – you'll probably find six for **A** and **E**, and five for **D** (the 6th string isn't played), but though in a way you're right, some notes are similar enough to be given the same name (these are said to be octaves apart). So basically these chords have three notes in them, though some are repeated; can you find the same notes further up the fingerboard (i.e. along the neck of the guitar towards the sound hole)?

All the chords you'll learn in this book (and many in the later ones) are the most "normal" sounding chords. Some are called "major" chords; like the ones you've learned so far.

Below I've shown another rhythm for you to try. Now you know the **A, D,** and **E** chords quite well, see if you can stop looking at your left hand, even when it changes chords. Then you can concentrate on what your right hand is doing. It's very important to get a steady rhythm. You'll also have time to give some attention to your singing.

Another Rhythm

The most common rhythm in modern music (in the West) is 4/4. Let's forget the second 4 again for the moment, and think about the first. What do you think the strumming pattern for this rhythm will be? Yes, you've guessed it. A heavy strum followed by three lighter ones. Let's try it . . .

4/4 Rhythm

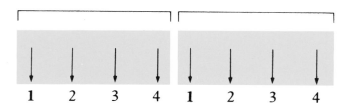

Count **1234, 1234,** etc. Stress the first-beat strum and follow with three lighter strums. Keep the strums evenly spaced, as before.

Melody Notes

The melody notes are the notes you sing. Try playing the single notes while a friend plays the chorus as shown. Or you can tape yourself playing the song and play along with that.

String	1st	2nd	1st	⌐2nd⌐	3rd	1st	⌐2nd⌐	1st
Fret	0	2	0	3	2	2 0	3	2 0

Kiss me and smile for me, tell me that you'll

⌐2nd⌐	3rd	1st	⌐2nd⌐	1st	⌐2nd⌐	3rd	⌐2nd⌐
3	2 2	0	3	2	0	3 2	2 2 0

wait for me Hold me like you'll never let me go,

⌐——1st——⌐	2nd	⌐1st⌐	2nd ⌐	1st	⌐	2nd	1st
0	0 0	2	2 0	3	0	0	2 0

'Cause I'm leaving on a jet plane, don't know when

2nd	1st	⌐2nd⌐	3rd	1st	⌐—2nd—⌐	3rd	2nd
3	0	3	2 2	0	3	2 0	2 0

I'll be back again Oh babe I hate to go . . .

Leaving On A Jet Plane John Denver

Accompaniment 4/4 Rhythm | = Strum Down   *V* = Verse   *C* = Chorus

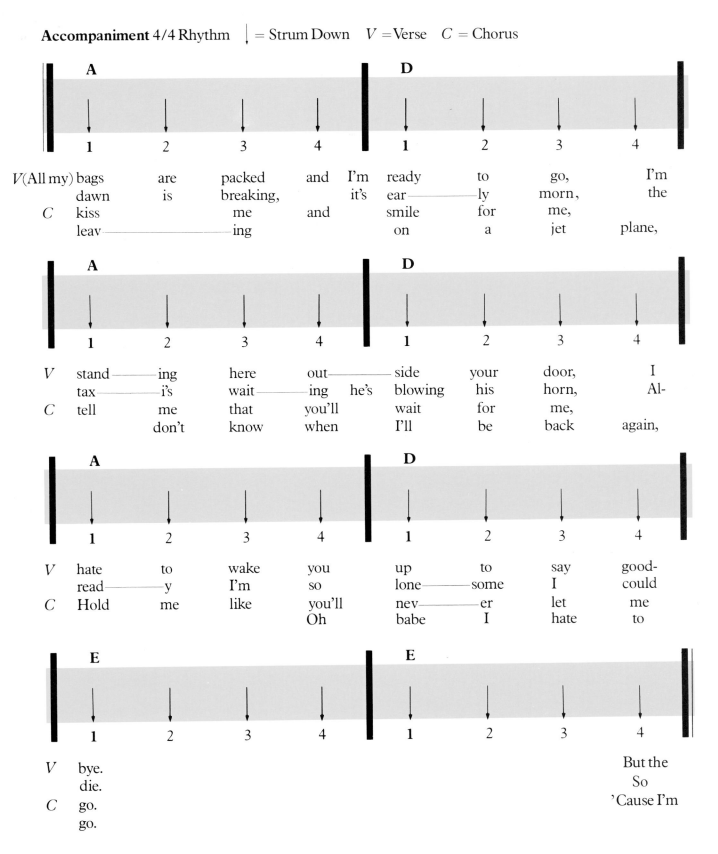

	A				D			
	1	2	3	4	1	2	3	4
V(All my)	bags	are	packed	and I'm	ready	to	go,	I'm
	dawn	is	breaking,	it's	ear———ly	morn,	me,	the
C	kiss	me	and	smile	for	a	jet	
	leav————————ing			on			plane,	

	A				D			
	1	2	3	4	1	2	3	4
V	stand———ing	here	out———side	your	door,	I	
	tax———i's	wait———ing he's	blowing	his	horn,	Al-	
C	tell	me	that you'll	wait	for	me,	
		don't	know when	I'll	be	back	again,	

	A				D			
	1	2	3	4	1	2	3	4
V	hate	to	wake	you	up	to	say	good-
	read———y	I'm	so	lone———some	I	could	
C	Hold	me	like	you'll	nev———er	let	me	
			Oh	babe	I	hate	to	

	E				E			
	1	2	3	4	1	2	3	4
V	bye.							But the
	die.							So
C	go.							'Cause I'm
	go.							

Note
The chord sequence is the same for each half of the
chorus as well as the verse, so sing the first lines of
words, then go on to the second lines and so on.

Blowin' In The Wind   Bob Dylan

Upstrokes

As we did with the 3/4 rhythm, let's add some upstrokes to the simple 4/4 pattern, and make things sound a bit more interesting. Finger an **E** chord and try several bars in a row with upstrokes between most beats . . .

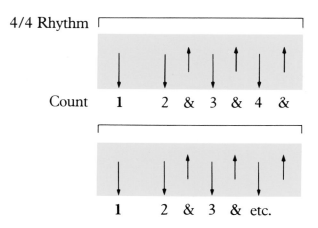

4/4 Rhythm

Count   1   2 & 3 & 4 &

1   2 & 3 & etc.

Because it's difficult to change chords cleanly when you have an upstroke at the end of a bar, I've removed this one in every bar of the accompaniment for "Blowin' In The Wind." Don't forget to keep a steady (and slow to start with) rhythm, each downstroke equally spaced whether or not there's an upstroke before or after it.

Melody Notes

Singing the first note of a song is not always easy. Find out which note in the chord is the one you sing for the first word (occasionally it's not a note in the chord that I show first but that doesn't matter. It makes for a much stronger beginning if you know exactly what note you're about to sing!).

When you get tired of playing the normal accompaniment, try playing the melody while a friend plays the chorus. Here are the notes of the chorus, with the string and fret shown, as before:

String	┌──2nd──┐			3rd	┌──2nd──┐			3rd
Fret	3	3	3	2	0	2	2	2	0	2

The answer, my friend, is blowin' in the wind,

┌──2nd──┐					┌─3rd─┐		
3	3	3	2	0	0	2	1	2

The answer is blowin' in the wind.

Lyrics

You'll notice that in almost all cases the words of the first verse are shown beneath the notation. Quite often parts of the song are very similar, so later words are put under the same bars of notation. This gives you less to remember. Later on you'll be trying many slight variations to make your guitar accompaniments more interesting.

Accompaniment 4/4 Rhythm   ↓↑ = Strum Down and Up

Verse

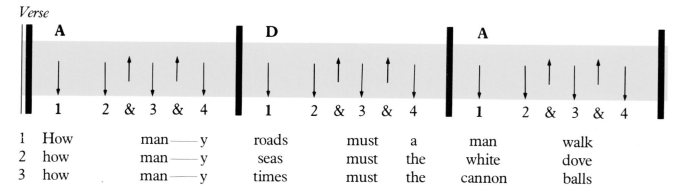

A						D						A					
1	2	&	3	&	4	1	2	&	3	&	4	1	2	&	3	&	4

1	How	man——y	roads	must	a	man	walk
2	how	man——y	seas	must	the	white	dove
3	how	man——y	times	must	the	cannon	balls

Blowin' In The Wind Continued

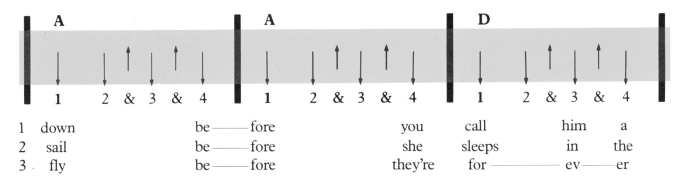

1	down	be ——— fore	you	call	him	a
2	sail	be ——— fore	she	sleeps	in	the
3 .	fly	be ——— fore	they're	for ——— ev ——— er

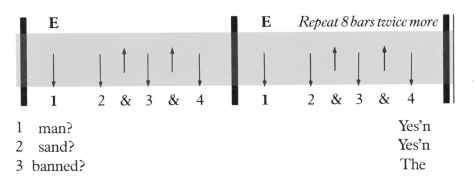

1 man?   Yes'n
2 sand?   Yes'n
3 banned?   The

Chorus

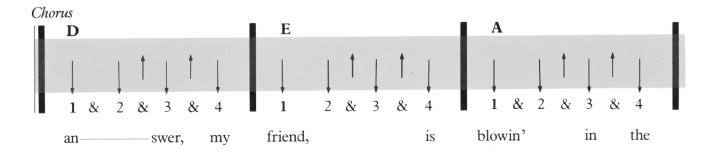

an———swer,   my   friend,   is   blowin'   in   the

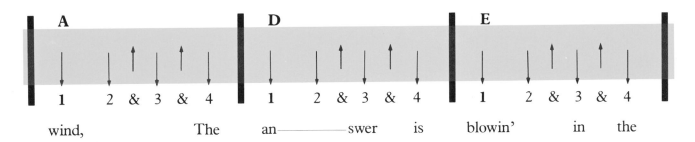

wind,   The   an———swer   is   blowin'   in   the

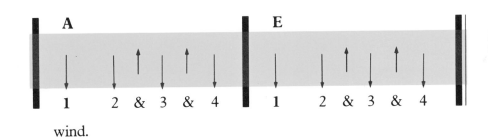

wind.

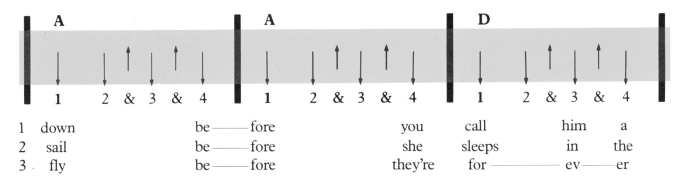

Strumming

Summary

Strum Patterns

Here are the 3/4 and 4/4 strum patterns you've already seen, plus a few more...

3/4 Rhythm (Any chord)

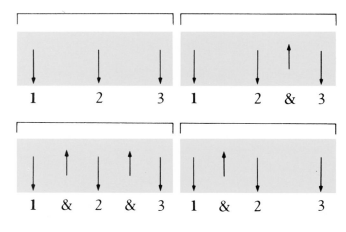

4/4 Rhythm (Any chord)

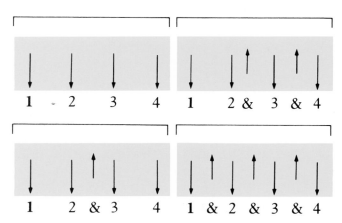

Play each of the above patterns over and over again, until your right hand can remember each of the rhythms easily.

Experiment with mixing these patterns up, and in the end you'll use different ones to get different effects, whenever you like. You'll notice that there are no upstrokes at the end of the patterns. For the moment you can put them in sometimes, but only when you're holding the same chord into the next bar. Otherwise it's quite hard to do an upstroke and change chords at the same time.

With an upstroke at the end, the second 3/4 pattern would be counted: 1, 2 & 3 &. Then you'd go straight into the first beat or downstrum of the next bar. Putting an upstroke at the end of the second 4/4 pattern, it would be counted: 1, 2 & 3 & 4 &.

Harmonies

Those of you who have a tape recorder and can remember tunes easily, could have a go at singing harmonies. Perhaps the best songs for this are those with a good chorus, like "Blowin' In The Wind."

Other Songs

Here are a few titles of songs that you can play using the patterns that are listed above. These are well known but more traditional pieces...

3/4
The Happy Birthday Song
My Bonnie Lies Over The Ocean
Irene Goodnight
Clementine

4/4
Michael Row The Boat Ashore
Listen To The Mocking Bird
Jingle Bells
Pick A Bale Of Cotton

How to Do It

The bass-strum style of playing is halfway between strumming and fingerpicking. Only your thumb on the right hand strikes individual strings, and the fingers brush across the treble strings. Normally the strums are shorter than in ordinary strumming. Let's have a look at the simple 3/4 and simple 4/4 patterns . . .

3/4 Rhythm (Finger an **A** Chord)

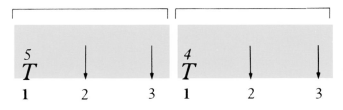

4/4 Rhythm (Finger an **E** Chord)

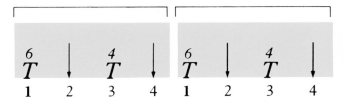

As you've guessed, the *T*s mean the thumb strikes. The number on top of the *T* means the string your thumb has to hit. In the patterns shown above, the thumb-strike replaces a downstrum on the first beat of every bar in the 3/4 rhythm. In the 4/4 bars, two downstrokes are replaced by thumb-strikes: the first and the third.

Count the bars as usual, keeping a steady rhythm. Don't move your right hand too much, or your thumb won't be in the right position for the next bass-string strike.

To begin with, the bass strings chosen to be hit when playing certain chords are the most usual. Try to remember which ones are the usual ones for the different chords you know.

Now have a look at some more songs.

Simple 4/4 Pattern Sequence (finger an **E** chord)

Thumb strikes 6th string

Strum down

Thumb strikes 4th string

Strum down

The Times They Are A-Changin' Warm Up

Two New Chords

When a song starts and ends with an **A** chord, it will have been played "in the key of **A**." The two other chords usually found with the **A** chord then are the **D** and **E** chords, as you've seen. When a song starts and ends with the **D** chord, the key will be **D**, and the other two chords generally found with the **D** chord will be the **A** and **G** chords. You already know the **A** chord, but quite often, when going back to the **D** chord, the **A** seventh (**A7** for short) will be used. So let's have a look at the **A7** and the **G** chords.

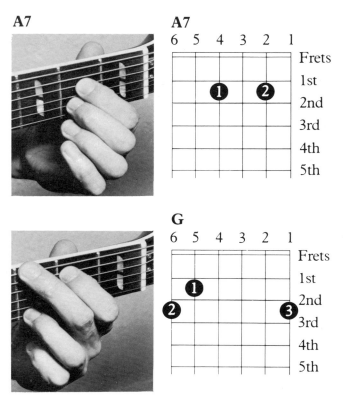

A7

A7

G

For the **A7,** start with the first finger on 4th string, 2nd fret. Same fret, 5th string for the **G**. Pull your third finger back so the tip rests on the first string properly. Keep the left-hand thumb on the middle of the back of the neck.

Upstrokes

You'll see that there are some upstrokes here and there, as well as a mixture of patterns. Use just one pattern to start with, if you like, and don't bother with the two-beat rest bar, play it as normal. Then play the song as shown, counting the two beats (or tap your foot) instead of playing them. You **do**

sing on the last beat of that bar, however. Small changes to the usual right-hand rhythm and pattern help to make the playing sound more interesting.

Right-Hand Position

When you're doing the ordinary strumming styles, there are no problems with moving your right hand away from the strings, unless you are playing at a fast tempo, or quick strokes are involved. But with the bass-strum style, the right hand must stay reasonably near the bass strings all the time, otherwise it won't be easy to hit the right string. So hold the thumb slightly to the left of the fingers, and make the strums (use all the fingers, held together, for the moment) quite short and sharp, especially the upstrokes. Make the thumb-strikes stand out.

The Times They Are A-Changin'   Bob Dylan

Accompaniment 3/4 Rhythm   ↓↑ = Strum down/up $\overset{4}{T}$ = Thumb plays 4th string

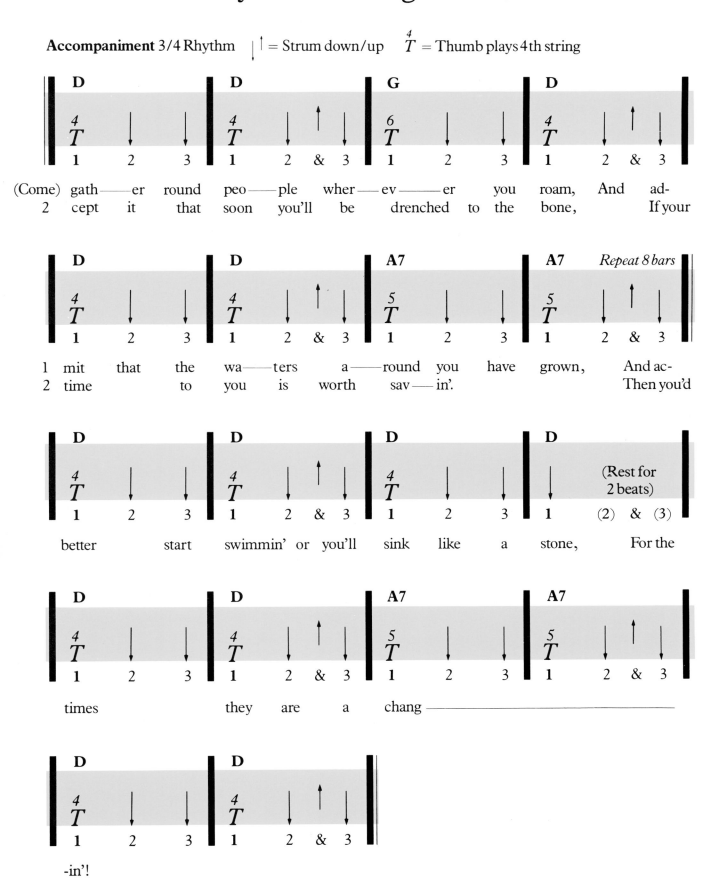

17

Colours Warm Up

Clean Playing

This is a reminder to those of you who may be blindly (or is it deafly?) bashing away, without really listening to the sort of sounds you and your guitar are producing. Can you answer Yes to these three questions?

Are you tuning your guitar every time you pick it up? If it's not in very good tune, however well you follow my directions the overall sound won't be very nice to listen to.

Are you pressing down hard enough with the left hand when you play? However well you do with your rhythm, it's your left hand that determines the quality of the sound that comes out. Try to **Practice a Little Each Day** and the ends of your fingers will harden up. Then you'll find it easy to press down.

Are your left-hand fingernails very short? Cut them regularly, and that'll help you press down on the strings properly. Don't let your fingers get too far from the metal strip (fret wire) either, and that'll help you get a clean sound. If you concentrate now, for a couple of weeks, on producing pure sounds, with little or no buzzing noises, after that you'll do it automatically. It's a good time to get rid of any bad habits!

Using the Capo

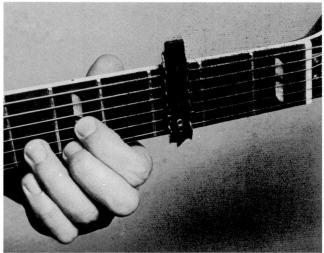

In my "useful information" notes at the start of the book, I mentioned the capo. If you find the melody of a song too low for you to sing comfortably, try using your capo.

In the picture above, a **D** chord (shape) is fingered, but with a capo placed on the 3rd fret. The capo effectively shortens the neck of the guitar and increases the pitch of all the strings by the same amount. This means that the capo can be treated as the end of the neck (i.e. as the 'nut') and the same shapes can be fingered.

The Bass Notes

For the **G** and **D** chords I've given the 3rd string as a bass-string strike. Though the 6th, 5th, and 4th strings are generally considered to be the bass strings, and the other three the treble, in this and other picking styles the 3rd is often used as part of the 'rhythm' rather than 'melody'. After hitting the 3rd string you should still hit it along with the others for the strum following.

Remember not to move your right hand too much in this style, and make the bass-strikes ring out.

Colours   Donovan

Accompaniment 4/4 Rhythm   ↓ = Strum down $\overset{4}{T}$ = Thumb plays 4th str.

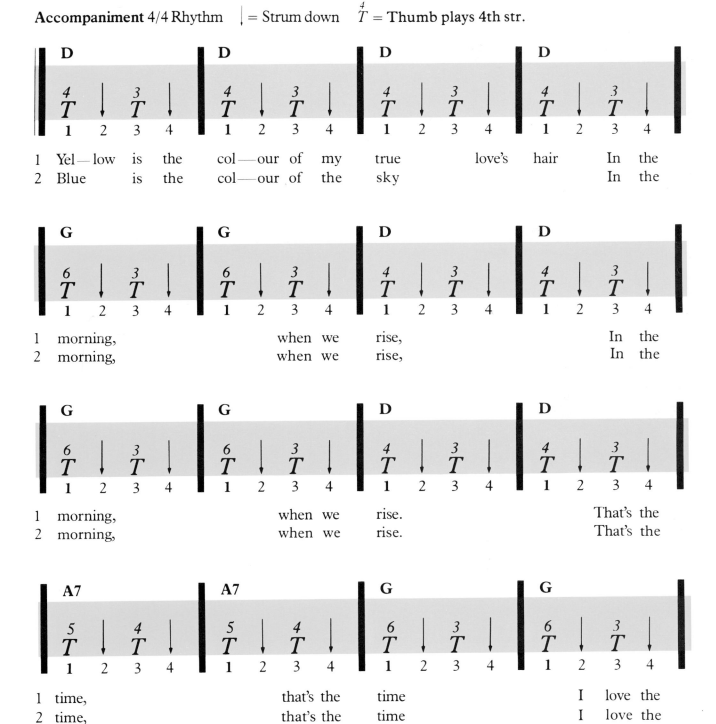

1 Yel—low is the col—our of my true love's hair In the
2 Blue is the col—our of the sky In the

1 morning, when we rise, In the
2 morning, when we rise, In the

1 morning, when we rise. That's the
2 morning, when we rise. That's the

1 time, that's the time I love the
2 time, that's the time I love the

1 best.
2 best.

19

Me And Bobby McGee Kris Kristofferson

Warm Up

This very long accompaniment isn't very difficult, but there are one or two things to look out for. I've varied the bass strings a little, but in all cases the

first bass note in a bar is the same for each of the three chords (5th for **A**, 6th for **E**, and 4th for **D** – these are the ones that almost always start for these chords).

Accompaniment 4/4 Rhythm $\downarrow\uparrow$ = Strum down/up $\overset{5}{T}$ = Thumb plays 5th string

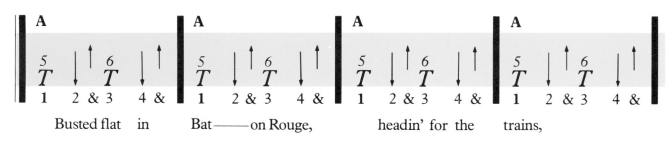

Busted flat in   Bat——on Rouge,   headin' for the   trains,

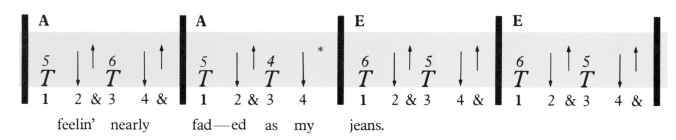

feelin' nearly   fad—ed   as   my   jeans.

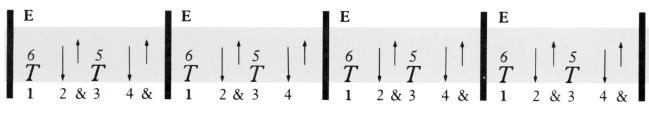

Bobby thumbed a   die— sel down,   just before it   rained,

Me And Bobby McGee Continued

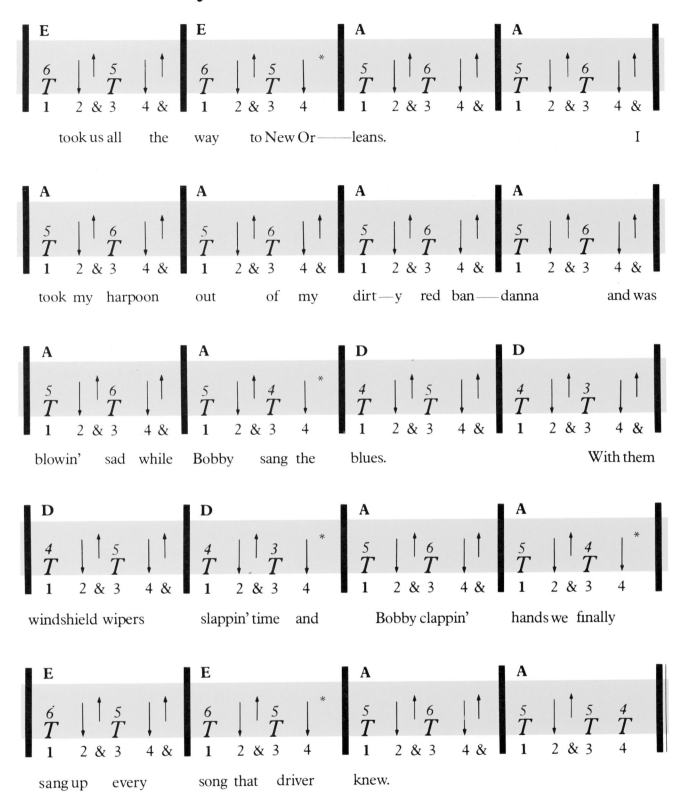

*The last upstroke before a chord change has been removed.

Summary

Bass – Strum Patterns

First let's go over the bass-strum patterns we've used.

3/4 (Finger a **D**)   3/4 (Finger a **G**)

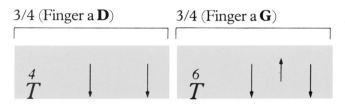

4/4(Finger an **A**) 4/4(Finger an **E**) 4/4(Finger an **A7**)

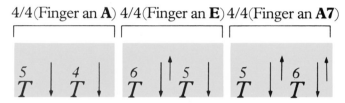

Did you count the rhythm correctly? Fine.

Now try these new patterns, which include the use of more thumb-strikes than the usual. Taking out or adding one or more upstrokes changes the feel of the rhythm a lot. Experiment!

3/4 (Finger a **D**) 3/4 (Finger an **A**)3/4 (Finger an **E**)

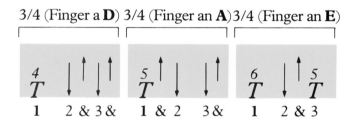

1   2 & 3 &   1 & 2   3 &   1   2 & 3

4/4 (Finger a **G**) 4/4 (Finger a **D**)4/4 (Finger an **A7**)

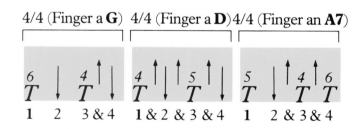

1   2   3 & 4   1 & 2 & 3 & 4   1   2 & 3 & 4

Using one or more of the above patterns, go back and play "Colours" with a more interesting accompaniment.

Bass – Pluck Style

A very similar style to the bass-strum one is the 'bass-pluck' style, which also uses the bass-string strikes as the key feature of the accompaniment. Instead of the strums, you pick all three treble strings together (pluck means an upward pick) with the first three right-hand fingers. The two simple 3/4 and 4/4 patterns work well for this style, and will sound fine for many traditional songs (see below).

Other Songs

Here are a few suggestions for songs to play in the bass-strum style, all of which can be played with just three chords. As a contrast to the modern ones I'm using, these are more traditional…

3/4
So Long, It's Been Good To Know You
On Top Of Old Smokey
Lavender's Blue
There's A Hole In The Bucket

4/4
Oh When The Saints Go Marching In
She'll Be Coming Round The Mountain
This Land Is Your Land
The Fox

How to Do It

This style of playing involves the thumb and first three fingers on the right hand. Let's take a look at one bar of the arpeggio style in 3/4 rhythm, followed by one in 4/4...

3/4 (Finger a **G**)   4/4 (Finger an **A**)

$$\overset{6}{T}\ i\ m\ r\ m\ i \qquad \overset{5}{T}\ i\ m\ r\ \overset{4}{T}\ i\ m\ r$$
1 & 2 & 3 &   1 & 2 & 3 & 4 &

In order to play the accompaniments that follow, you must remember that:
the *Index* finger (first) always plays the **3rd String,**
the *Middle* finger (second) always plays the **2nd String,**
the *Ring* finger (third) always plays the **1st String.**

So the letters *i, m,* and *r* stand for index, middle, and ring fingers on the right hand.
As before, the large *T* and the small number on top of it stand for the thumb-strike and which string to play.

Hold your three fingers over the top three (treble) strings, and pluck them in the order shown above, after the thumb-strike. Don't get your fingers caught under the strings by trying to play too hard. This style is usually for slow songs and ballads, so hit the strings gently.

Can you play the above two bars smoothly?
Right, have a go at a few more songs...

Simple 4/4 Pattern Sequence (Finger an **A** chord)

Thumb strikes 5th string

Index finger strikes 3rd string

Middle finger strikes 2nd string

Ring finger strikes 1st string

Repeat above sequence to complete a bar, but starting with a 4th string thumb-strike.

23

Scarborough Fair Warm Up

Minor Chords

So far you've learned some major chords (and one seventh chord) which we've used to play in the major keys of A and D. Now here are two minor chords that are very easy to play, and which give a very different flavor to an accompaniment . . .

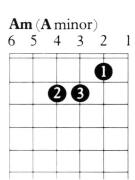

Am (**A** minor)

Em (**E** minor)

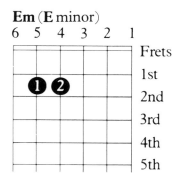

Finger the **A** (major) chord and then the **Am**. What's the difference between them? Now finger the **E** (major) chord and follow it with the **Em**. What's the difference between them? Yes, there's only one note that changes, and that note only changes by one fret. Taking this note down by one fret causes the chord to sound rather sad.

Try some changes from the major chords to the minor ones, then you'll be more prepared for this next song, "Scarborough Fair," which Paul Simon (with Art Garfunkel) made famous. But it was originally an English traditional song. Here the arrangement is in the key of A minor.

Helpful Hints

To begin with, play the thumb-strike quite hard, and make the treble notes softer. Play slowly and count the time carefully, then speed up when your fingers are flowing smoothly and you can remember all the chord changes and the words.

Near the end of the accompaniment you'll see a bar where there's only one strum, on the first beat. Play that strum right across all the strings, deliberately and not too fast. Then rest for two beats while singing "love of" on those two beats. After that you're back to the usual pattern for two bars of **Am** before beginning the next verse. Don't forget to use the capo to suit your vocal range.

24

Melody Notes

Here are the melody notes for you to check that you've got the tune right, and for playing along with the accompaniment given. Also try using a strumming bass pattern against the arpeggio. They should sound pretty good together.

Strings	⌐3rd¬	⌐1st¬	⌐2nd¬	3rd
Frets	2 2	0 0 0 0	1 0	2

Are you going to Scarborough Fair?

⌐1st¬	2nd	1st
0 3 5	3 0 2	3 0

Parsley, sage, rosemary, and thyme.

⌐1st¬	⌐2nd¬	3rd
5 5 5 3 0 0 0	3 1 0	2 0

Remember me to the one who lives there,

3rd 1st	⌐2nd¬	⌐3rd¬
2 0	3 1 0	2 0 2

she once was a true love of mine.

Scarborough Fair
Traditional, arranged Russ Shipton

Accompaniment 3/4 Rhythm $\overset{5}{T}$ = Thumb plays 5th string   *i m r* = index, middle, and ring fingers play 3rd, 2nd, and 1st strings

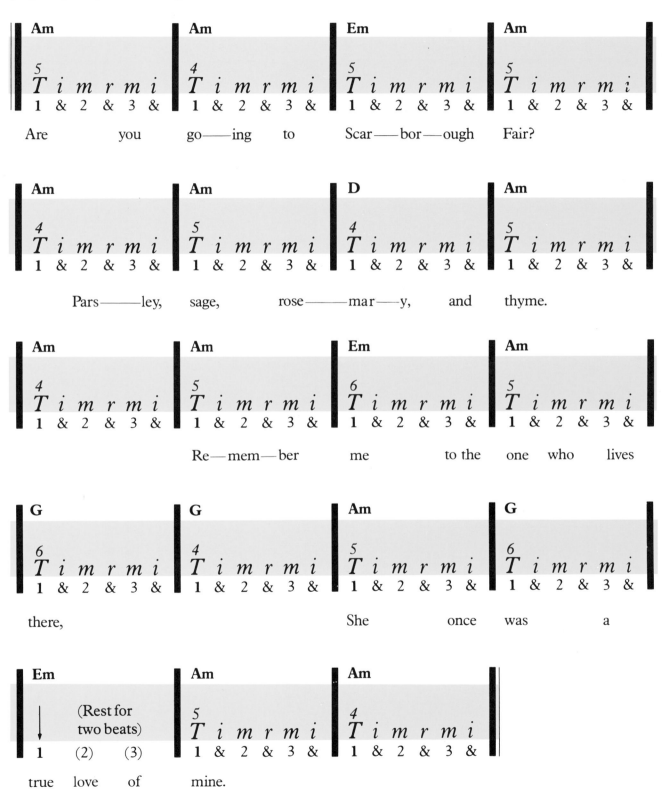

Note
Watch the bass strings very closely – I've varied them more than usual.

English Country Garden Warm Up

Another Seventh Chord

When you can manage the accompaniment given on the next page, try using this **E7** chord instead of the normal **E** – but only on the "gar – den" bars. You'll find that the change from **E7** to the **A** chord has a very final sound about it, and these bars are suited to this more than the other **E** bars. It also makes a nice alternative to the normal major chord. When you start picking your own songs to play, and trying out different chords, you'll find yourself choosing them on the basis of what sounds best to your ear, and for reasons of variety.

Like the **A7** chord moving to **D** (the 'tonic' or 'key' chord), the **E7** pulls strongly to the **A** chord. This is your first chord that has used all four fingers, but it's not very difficult, is it?

You'll see that the thumb-strikes are the same, but the ring finger plucks first, followed by the middle and then the index finger (each finger plays the same string as before, of course). It's strange at first, but worth mastering so you can get variety in this style. Now try playing "English Country Garden" with the new pattern.

Alternative Styles

After playing the accompaniment in the arpeggio style, rearrange it and see what it sounds like in the other two styles you know – strumming and bass strum. In the classroom, different groups can play the alternative styles at the same time. At home you can play along with a tape recording of a different style.

E7

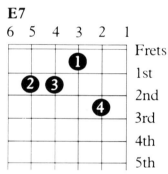

E7

	6	5	4	3	2	1	
				①			Frets
		②	③				1st
					④		2nd
							3rd
							4th
							5th

Alternative Pattern

If you're finding the accompaniment on the next page too easy, try "reversing" the treble strings, and do this kind of pattern . . .

A				**D**			
5				4			
T	*r*	*m*	*i*	*T*	*r*	*m*	*i*
1	&	2	&	3	&	4	&

E				**A**			
6				5			
T	*r*	*m*	*i*	*T*	*r*	*m*	*i*
1	&	2	&	3	&	4	&

English Country Garden

The Arpeggio Style

Accompaniment 4/4 Rhythm,   *T i m r* = Thumb, index, middle, and ring fingers

A				D				E				A			
5				4				6				5			
T	*i*	*m*	*r*	*T*	*i*	*m*	*r*	*T*	*i*	*m*	*r*	*T*	*i*	*m*	*r*
1	&	2	&	3	&	4	&	1	&	2	&	3	&	4	&

1 How man—y gen———tle flow ———— ers grow in an
2 I'll tell you now of some that I know and those I

A				D				E				A			*Repeat 4 bars*
4				4				6				5			
T	*i*	*m*	*r*	*T*	*i*	*m*	*r*	*T*	*i*	*m*	*r*	*T*	*i*	*m*	*r*
1	&	2	&	3	&	4	&	1	&	2	&	3	&	4	&

1 Eng———lish coun———try gar ——— den? (to the 2nd line)
2 miss you'll sure———ly par ——— don.

A				E				A				E			
5				6				5				6			
T	*i*	*m*	*r*	*T*	*i*	*m*	*r*	*T*	*i*	*m*	*r*	*T*	*i*	*m*	*r*
1	&	2	&	3	&	4	&	1	&	2	&	3	&	4	&

Daff—o—dils, heartsease, and flocks, meadow sweet, and lilies, stocks,

A				D				E				E			
5				4				6				5			
T	*i*	*m*	*r*	*T*	*i*	*m*	*r*	*T*	*i*	*m*	*r*	*T*	*i*	*m*	*r*
1	&	2	&	3	&	4	&	1	&	2	&	3	&	4	&

gen———tle lu———pine and tall holly———hocks, Roses,

A				D				E				A			
5				4				6				5			
T	*i*	*m*	*r*	*T*	*i*	*m*	*r*	*T*	*i*	*m*	*r*	*T*	*i*	*m*	*r*
1	&	2	&	3	&	4	&	1	&	2	&	3	&	4	&

fox———gloves, snow———drops, forget——me——nots, in an

A				D				E				A			
4				4				6				5			
T	*i*	*m*	*r*	*T*	*i*	*m*	*r*	*T*	*i*	*m*	*r*	*T*	*i*	*m*	*r*
1	&	2	&	3	&	4	&	1	&	2	&	3	&	4	&

Eng———lish coun———try gar ——— den.

The Last Thing On My Mind Tom Paxton

More Thumb-Strikes

This beautiful ballad from Tom Paxton gives you more practice at getting a smooth, gentle, arpeggio picking style. When you're happy with the pattern that's given, try changing the order of the treble strings and see what it sounds like. Then you can do this pattern, which includes another thumb-strike in each bar:

D		G	
4	5	6	5
T i m r m i T i		*T i m r m i T i*	
1 & 2 & 3 & 4 &		1 & 2 & 3 & 4 &	

Sounds pretty good, doesn't it? Now play the whole accompaniment with this kind of pattern.

General

The chorus of this song is perfect for harmonizing, so in the classroom the confident singers among you can try to sing a harmony line while the others sing the melody. At home, you can sing a harmony to the melody you've recorded. Give it a go, it's not so difficult!

If any of you are finding this arpeggio business a bit easy, see if you can find the melody notes of the chorus on your guitar.

Accompaniment 4/4 Rhythm,   *T i m r* = Thumb, index, middle, and ring fingers

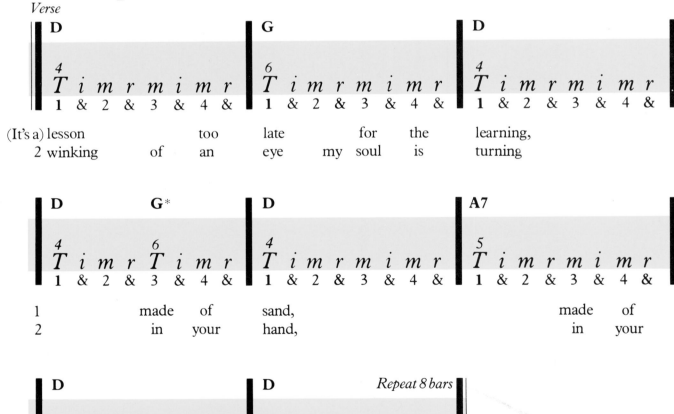

Verse

D	G	D
4	6	4
T i m r m i m r	*T i m r m i m r*	*T i m r m i m r*
1 & 2 & 3 & 4 &	1 & 2 & 3 & 4 &	1 & 2 & 3 & 4 &

(It's a) lesson .... too ... late .... for ... the .... learning,
2 winking ..... of ... an .... eye ... my soul ... is .... turning

D G*	D	A7
4 6	4	5
T i m r T i m r	*T i m r m i m r*	*T i m r m i m r*
1 & 2 & 3 & 4 &	1 & 2 & 3 & 4 &	1 & 2 & 3 & 4 &

1 .... made ... of ... sand, ... made ... of
2 .... in ... your ... hand, ... in ... your

D	D	*Repeat 8 bars*
4	4	
T i m r m i m r	*T i m r m i m r*	
1 & 2 & 3 & 4 &	1 & 2 & 3 & 4 &	

1 sand. .... In the
2 hand. .... Are ... you ... *(to Chorus, next page)*

*Watch out for this quick chord change!

The Last Thing On My Mind continued

Chorus

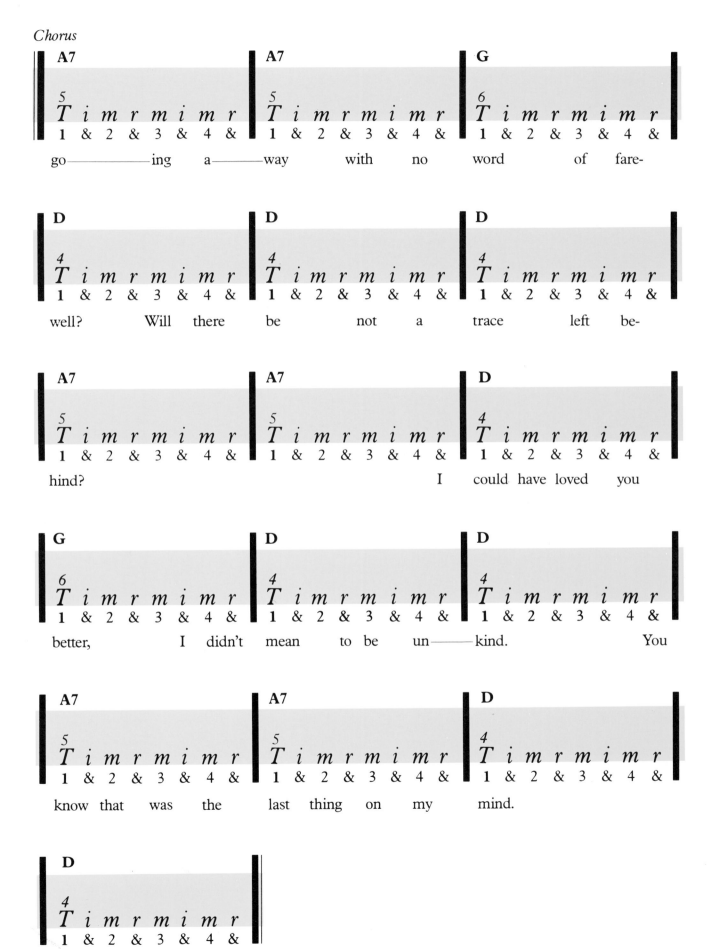

A7	A7	G
5 *T i m r m i m r*	5 *T i m r m i m r*	6 *T i m r m i m r*
1 & 2 & 3 & 4 &	1 & 2 & 3 & 4 &	1 & 2 & 3 & 4 &
go————ing a———way	with no	word of fare-

D	D	D
4 *T i m r m i m r*	4 *T i m r m i m r*	4 *T i m r m i m r*
1 & 2 & 3 & 4 &	1 & 2 & 3 & 4 &	1 & 2 & 3 & 4 &
well? Will there	be not a	trace left be-

A7	A7	D
5 *T i m r m i m r*	5 *T i m r m i m r*	4 *T i m r m i m r*
1 & 2 & 3 & 4 &	1 & 2 & 3 & 4 &	1 & 2 & 3 & 4 &
hind?	I	could have loved you

G	D	D
6 *T i m r m i m r*	4 *T i m r m i m r*	4 *T i m r m i m r*
1 & 2 & 3 & 4 &	1 & 2 & 3 & 4 &	1 & 2 & 3 & 4 &
better, I didn't	mean to be un———kind.	You

A7	A7	D
5 *T i m r m i m r*	5 *T i m r m i m r*	4 *T i m r m i m r*
1 & 2 & 3 & 4 &	1 & 2 & 3 & 4 &	1 & 2 & 3 & 4 &
know that was the	last thing on my	mind.

D
4 *T i m r m i m r*
1 & 2 & 3 & 4 &

29

The Arpeggio Style

Summary

Arpeggio Patterns

Here's another look at all the arpeggio patterns we've used . . .

3/4 (Finger **A**)   4/4 (Finger **G**)

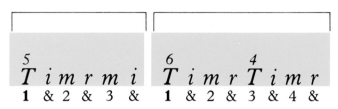

4/4 (Finger **D** then **G**)

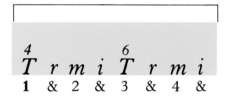

4/4 (Finger **Am**)

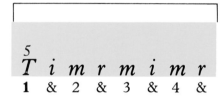

4/4 (Finger **Em**)

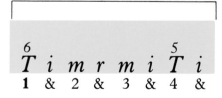

Did you count the rhythm correctly? Fine – now try these two 3/4 patterns that use similar ideas to the 4/4 ones:

3/4 (Finger **G**)   3/4 (Finger **Am**)

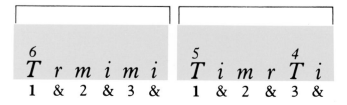

Now here's one pattern of each rhythm that has slight differences to the others you've played . . .

3/4 (Finger **A**)   4/4 (Finger **Em**)

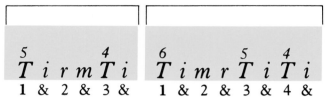

Play the same pattern over and over again till it's smooth.

Other Songs

Most of the slower, ballad-type songs are suitable for the arpeggio style accompaniment. Here are a few (again more traditional) other songs that you might like to try – they can all be played with three chords or less.

3/4
Home On The Range
Oh Dear, What Can The Matter Be?
Down In The Valley
I Never Will Marry

4/4
All My Trials
Kum Ba Yah
Rambler, Gambler
The Riddle Song

Amazing Grace

Verse 1:
Amazing grace, how sweet the sound
That saved a wretch like me.
I once was lost but now I'm found,
Was blind but now I see.
Verse 2:
'Twas grace that taught my heart to fear
And grace my fear relieved.
How precious did that grace appear
The hour I first believed.
Verse 3:
Through many dangers, toils and snares
We have already come.
'Twas grace that brought us safe thus far
And grace will lead us home.
Verse 4:
We've been there ten thousand years
Bright, shining as the sun.
We've no less days to sing God's praise
Than when we first begun.

Catch The Wind

Verse 1:
In the chilly hours and minutes of uncertainty
I want to be
In the warm hold of your lovin' mind.
To feel you all around me and to take your hand
Along the sand,
Ah, but I may as well try and catch the wind!
Verse 2:
When sundown pales the sky, I want to hide
awhile
Behind your smile
And everywhere I'd look your eyes I'd find.
For me to love you now would be the sweetest
thing,
'Twould make me sing,
Ah, but I may as well try and catch the wind!
Verse 3:
When rain has hung the leaves with tears, I want
you near
To kill my fears,
To help me to leave all my blues behind.
Standin' in your heart is where I want to be
And long to be,
Ah, but I may as well try and catch the wind!

Leaving On A Jet Plane

Verse 1:
All my bags are packed and I'm ready to go, I'm
standing here outside your door,
I hate to wake you up to say goodbye.
But the dawn is breaking, it's early morn, the taxi's
waiting he's blowin' his horn,
Already I'm so lonesome I could die.
Chorus:
So kiss me and smile for me, tell me that you'll
wait for me,
Hold me like you'll never let me go.
'Cause I'm leaving on a jet plane, don't know when
I'll be back again,
Oh babe I hate to go.
Verse 2:
There's so many times I've let you down, so many
times I've played around,
I tell you now, they don't mean a thing.
Every place I go I'll think of you, every song I sing
I'll sing for you,
When I come back, I'll wear your wedding ring.
Verse 3:
Well now the time has come to leave you, one more
time please let me kiss you,
Then close your eyes and I'll be on my way.
Dream about the days to come, when I won't have
to leave you alone
About the times I won't have to say:

Blowin' In The Wind

Verse 1:
How many roads must a man walk down before
you call him a man?
Yes'n how many seas must the white dove sail
before she sleeps in the sand?
Yes 'n how many times must the cannon balls fly
before they're forever banned?
Chorus:
The answer, my friend, is blowin' in the wind,
The answer is blowin' in the wind.
Verse 2:
How many times must a man look up before he
can see the sky?
Yes'n how many ears must one man have before
he can hear people cry?
Yes'n how many deaths will it take till he knows
that too many people have died?

Verse 3:
How many years can a mountain exist before it is washed to the sea?
Yes'n how many years can some people exist before they're allowed to be free?
Yes'n how many times can a man turn his head pretending he just doesn't see?

The Times They Are A-Changin'

Verse 1:
Come gather round people, wherever you roam,
And admit that the waters around you have grown,
And accept it that soon you'll be drenched to the bone,
If your time to you is worth savin'.
Then you'd better start swimmin' or you'll sink like a stone,
For the times they are a changin'!
Verse 2:
Come writers and critics who prophesy with your pen,
And keep your eyes wide, the chance won't come again,
And don't speak too soon for the wheel's still in spin,
And there's no tellin' who that it's namin'.
For the loser now will be later to win,
For the times they are a-changin'!
Verse 3:
Come senators, congressmen, please heed the call.
Don't stand in the doorway, don't block up the hall.
For he that gets hurt will be he who has stalled.
There's a battle outside and it's ragin'.
It'll soon shake your windows and rattle your walls
For the times they are a-changin'!
Verse 4:
Come mothers and fathers throughout the land,
And don't criticise what you can't understand.
Your sons and your daughters are beyond your command.
Your old road is rapidly agin'.
Please get out of the new one if you can't lend your hand,
For the times they are a-changin'!
Verse 5:
The line it is drawn the curse it is cast.
The slow one now will later be fast.
As the present now will later be past.
The order is rapidly fadin'.
And the first one now will later be last,
For the times they are a-changin'!

Colours

Verse 1:
Yellow is the colour of my true love's hair
In the morning, when we rise,
In the morning, when we rise.
That's the time, that's the time
I love the best.
Verse 2:
Blue is the colour of the sky
In the morning, when we rise,
In the morning, when we rise.
That's the time, that's the time
I love the best.
Verse 3:
Green is the colour of the sparklin' corn
In the morning, when we rise,
In the morning, when we rise.
That's the time, that's the time
I love the best.
Verse 4:
Mellow is the feelin' that I get
When I see her, mm hmm,
When I see her, uh huh.
That's the time, that's the time
I love the best.
Verse 5:
Freedom is a word I rarely use
Without thinkin', mm hmm,
Without thinkin', mm hmm,
Of the time, of the time
When I've been loved.

Me And Bobby McGee

Verse 1:
Busted flat in Baton Rouge, headin' for the trains, feelin' nearly faded as my jeans.
Bobby thumbed a diesel down, just before it rained, took us all the way to New Orleans.
I took my harpoon out of my dirty red bandanna and was blowin' sad while Bobby sang the blues.
With them windshield wipers slappin' time and Bobby clappin' hands we finally sang up every song that driver knew.
1st chorus:
Freedom's just another word for nothin' left to lose, and nothin' ain't worth nothin' but it's free.
Feelin' good was easy, Lord, when Bobby sang the blues, and buddy, that was good enough for me,
Good enough for me and my Bobby McGee.

Verse 2:
From the coal mines of Kentucky to the California sun, Bobby shared the secrets of my soul,
Standin' right beside me through everythin' I done, and every night she kept me from the cold.
Then somewhere near Salinas, Lord, I let her slip away, she was lookin' for the love I hoped she'd find.
Well I'd trade all my tomorrows for a single yesterday, holdin' Bobby's body close to mine.
2nd chorus:
Freedom's just another word for nothin' left to lose, and nothin' left was all she left for me.
Feelin' good was easy, Lord, when Bobby sang the blues, and buddy, that was good enough for me,
Good enough for me and Bobby McGee.

Scarborough Fair

Verse 1:
Are you going to Scarborough Fair?
Parsley, sage, rosemary, and thyme.
Remember me to the one who lives there,
She once was a true love of mine.
Verse 2:
Tell her to make me a cambric shirt:
Parsley, sage, rosemary, and thyme.
Without any seams nor needle work,
Then she'll be a true love of mine.
Verse 3:
Tell her to find me an acre of land:
Parsley, sage, rosemary, and thyme.
Between the salt-water and the sea strand,
Then she'll be a true love of mine.
Verse 4:
Tell her to plough it with sickle of leather:
Parsley, sage, rosemary, and thyme.
And bind it all in a bunch of heather,
Then she'll be a true love of mine.

English Country Garden

Verse 1:
How many gentle flowers grow in an English country garden?
I'll tell you now of some that I know and those I miss you'll surely pardon:
Daffodils, heartsease, and flocks, meadow sweet, and lilies, stocks, gentle lupine, and tall hollyhocks,
Roses, foxgloves, snowdrops, forget-me-nots, in an English country garden.

Verse 2:
How many insects find their home in an English country garden?
I'll tell you now of some that I know and those I miss you'll surely pardon:
Dragonflies, moths, and bees, spiders falling from the trees.
Butterflies sway in the mild, gentle breeze.
There are hedgehogs that roam and little gnomes in an English country garden.
Verse 3:
How many songbirds make their nests in an English country garden?
I'll tell you now of some that I know and those I miss you'll surely pardon:
Babbling coo, cooing doves, robins, and the warbling thrush,
Bluebird, lark, finch, and nightingale.
We all smile in the spring, when the birds all start to sing
In an English country garden.

The Last Thing On My Mind

Verse 1:
It's a lesson too late for the learning, made of sand, made of sand.
In the winking of an eye my soul is turning in your hand, in your hand.
Chorus:
Are you going away with no word of farewell?
Will there be not a trace left behind?
I could have loved you better, I didn't mean to be unkind.
You know that was the last thing on my mind.
Verse 2:
You've got reason aplenty for going, this I know, this I know.
For the weeds have been steadily growing, please don't go, please don't go.
Verse 3:
As I lie in my bed in the morning without you, without you,
Each song in my breast dies a-borning without you, without you.
Verse 4:
As I walk down the street the subway's rumbling underground, underground,
While the thoughts in my head they're a-tumbling round and round, round and round.

Congratulations! You've reached the end of the first book. You're no longer a "beginner," and the hardest part is over.

Now you know eight chords and various patterns in three quite different right-hand styles. This is a good basis for developing a broad ability in guitar playing.

Some of you may have been playing the guitar for a while before using this book, so you may have found it easier than the others did, but there's always something to gain from any new material. Don't pass over things too quickly. You might not know them as well as you think.

In the second, third, and fourth books I'll gradually explain more music theory, and introduce more single-note, classical pieces, so you have some idea of how the different types of music are related. Those of you who have already studied some music theory should try to tie in your knowledge with what you've been playing on the guitar. A little musical knowledge helps greatly in arranging material quickly and increasing your repertoire.

Before going on to the next book, try to find some songs that can be played with the chords you know, and experiment with the various right-hand styles and patterns. Then I want you to remember the 'open-string' notes (i.e. when no finger is on a fret) of the guitar . . .

E	A	D	G	B	E	Notes
6	5	4	3	2	1	String Numbers

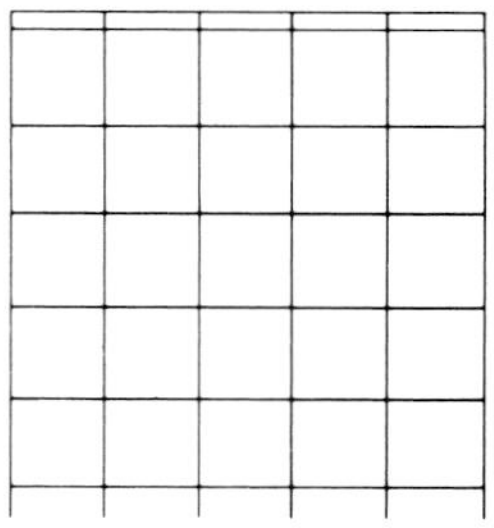

Frets
1st
2nd
3rd
4th
5th

Have you committed the open-string notes to memory? Good – see you in Book 2, for some great songs and interesting things to learn!

The Complete Guitar Player

by Russ Shipton.

Songs and music in this book
Drunken Sailor
Freight Train
The House Of The Risin' Sun
If I Were A Carpenter
Maxwell's Silver Hammer
Ob-la-di Ob-la-da
Sailing
Study: Fernando Sor
This Land Is Your Land
Yellow Submarine

Amsco Publications   New York/London/Sydney/Cologne

Music Theory

So you can understand the sheet music of any songs you want to learn and play on your guitar, you must be able to read the melody notes as they're shown on the 'treble clef'. If you don't know, or aren't sure exactly how this standard musical notation works, go carefully through this page – and don't start thinking it's difficult – it's quite easy, and follows simple rules!

The first seven letters of the alphabet are used, but the intervals between them are not the same . . .

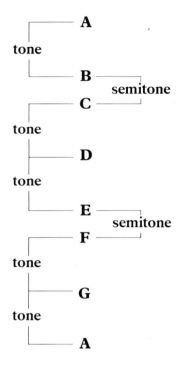

Between the notes **E** and **F**, and **B** and **C**, there is no intermediary note. Between the others there is a note that's called 'sharp' or 'flat.' In other words, the note between **A** and **B** may be called **A♯** (sharp) or **B♭** (flat). Can you guess the note between **F** and **G**? Yes, that's right, **F♯** or **G♭**.

Music Notation

The top line of music in the song sheet or book you buy is the melody. Have a look at the treble clef and where you can find the notes . . .

This is the old sign for **G**. It signifies the treble clef

A B C D E F G A B C D E

This is the 'middle **C**' (the **C** note in the middle of the piano). It's the 1st fret, 2nd string on the guitar, but **guitar music is shown an octave higher than actually played.**

A note is sharped (made a semitone higher) or flatted (made a semitone lower) with a sign placed **either** at the start of the line **or** just before it, like this . . .

As well as the 'pitch' (higher or lower) of the notes, the music notation will tell you how long the notes last. Here are the main signs that indicate the length of time each note should last when the time sign has a "4" below...

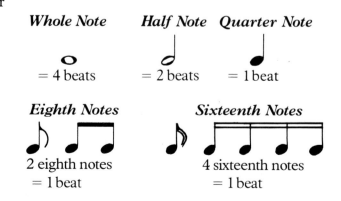

Whole Note 𝅝 = 4 beats

Half Note = 2 beats

Quarter Note = 1 beat

Eighth Notes 2 eighth notes = 1 beat

Sixteenth Notes 4 sixteenth notes = 1 beat

Swing Rhythm

Some songs sound great with a "swing" rhythm, and all the patterns you've learned so far can be swung, as long as there are strums or notes between the beats. All you have to do is to **delay the upstroke** (or note between the beat) until **just before** the following beat or downstroke. Try to lengthen the downstrokes and shorten the upstrokes in this simple pattern (play any chord).

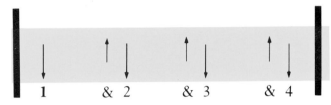

It may help you to count the bar like this: 1, &2, &3, &4.

Stops

You'll notice some rests in two of the songs in this section – just tap your foot for each beat, and you'll have no trouble. It's good to break up the accompaniment on many songs like this, because it makes the overall sound more interesting and effective.

Final Upstrokes

All players using strumming accompaniments make strokes on the half-beat, just before the left hand changes chords (it helps to keep both the rhythm and sound going). And almost always the sound produced is rather muffled, because the left hand is actually moving when the right hand strikes – so don't worry too much about getting a clear note on these upstrokes. But **make sure** your left hand is in the new chord position for the first downstroke.

Finding the Melody

Most of you will have been over the music theory I've briefly shown on the opposite page, in earlier school music classes, or during private sessions. Check it through again, and be sure you understand these basic ideas – gathering and arranging songs is much easier when you know them.

So before you have fun with the three Beatles songs in this section, check the melody of each one first. That means you'll have to put your theory into practice by working out the notes on the treble clef. If you have a copy, it will help you to refer to these songs in **The Complete Guitar Player Songbook.** When you've worked out the notes, find them on the guitar; this fretboard diagram should help you . . .

The Fretboard (or Fingerboard)

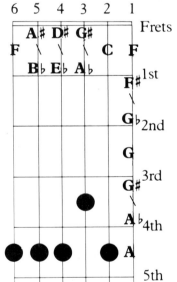

One piano key to the next = 1 Semitone
One guitar fret to the next = 1 Semitone

You'll see that moving toward the body of the guitar one fret at a time, the note goes up by one semitone at a time. So each fret of the guitar is equal to one semitone – i.e. one piano key, whether black or white.

Try filling in the other notes on the first five frets of the fretboard . . .

Yellow Submarine Lennon/McCartney

We're starting this second book with a few Beatles songs, and they're all quite easy to play. This one involves the swing strum rhythm that we went over in the warm up for this section, and only three

chords – can you remember **Am**? Good, now try this accompaniment, and watch out for the slight pattern changes I've made in the chorus.

Accompaniment 4/4 Swing Rhythm   ↓↑ = Strum down/up

Verse

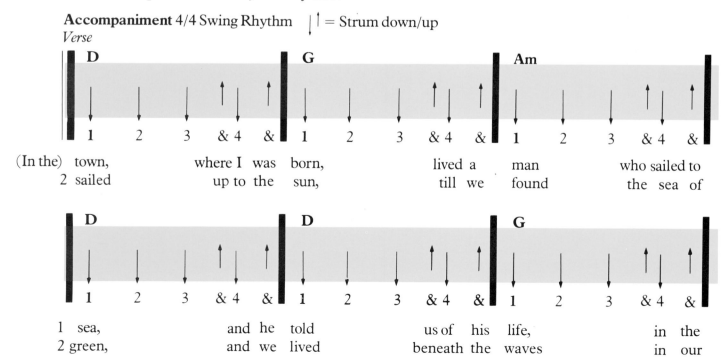

| | D | | | | | G | | | | | Am | | | | | D | | | | | D | | | | | G | | | | |

(In the) town,   where I was born,   lived a man   who sailed to
2 sailed   up to the sun,   till we found   the sea of

1 sea,   and he told   us of his life,   in the
2 green,   and we lived   beneath the waves   in our

6

Yellow Submarine Continued

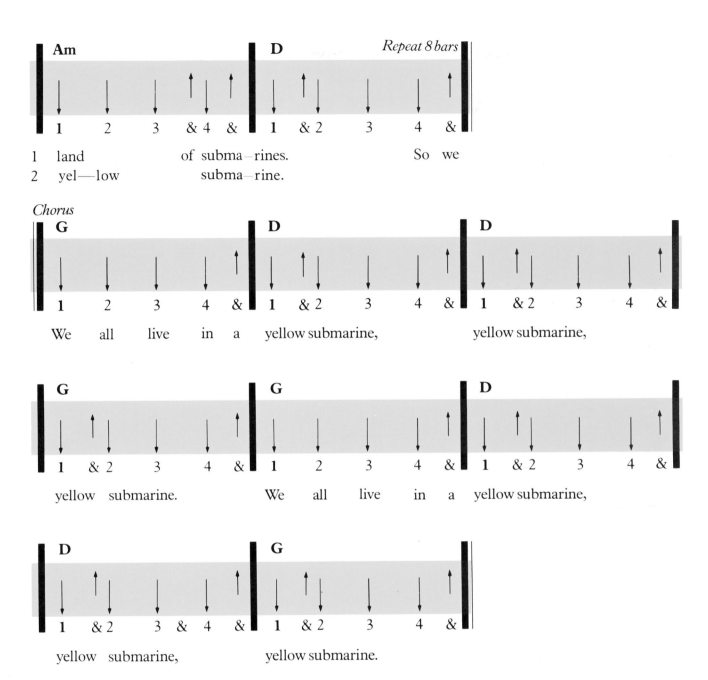

Am	D	*Repeat 8 bars*
1 2 3 & 4 &	1 & 2 3 4 &	
1 land of subma—rines.	So we	
2 yel—low subma—rine.		

Chorus

G	D	D
1 2 3 4 &	1 & 2 3 4 &	1 & 2 3 4 &
We all live in a	yellow submarine,	yellow submarine,

G	G	D
1 & 2 3 4 &	1 2 3 4 &	1 & 2 3 4 &
yellow submarine.	We all live in a	yellow submarine,

D	G
1 & 2 3 & 4 &	1 & 2 3 4 &
yellow submarine,	yellow submarine.

Melody Notes

Check the melody of "Yellow Submarine." If you have a copy of **The Complete Guitar Player Songbook,** you will find this song in it. Try to find the notes shown on the treble clef on the guitar. Then sing them as you play them.

You may have noticed that unlike the piano and other instruments, on the guitar you can find the **same notes in several different places**. The open first string is an **E** note, for instance, and it can also be found on the 5th fret of the 2nd string, the 9th fret of the 3rd string, and the 14th fret of the 4th string.

I want you to choose the **lowest position.** In other words, the lowest in fret number (the lowest being an open string, of course). Then by sticking to just the lower area of the fretboard, it will give you a chance of remembering the positions of some notes more easily – after a while you'll be able to find and play the melody notes very quickly.

7

Maxwell's Silver Hammer   Lennon/McCartney

Another world-famous Beatles song, and this one also has a swing strum accompaniment. Before we go any further, have a go at these two new chords:

B Seventh   **F♯** Diminished

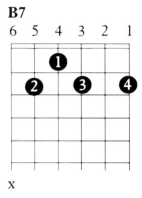
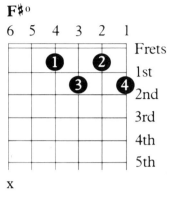

They both use all four fingers, but they're not too difficult, are they? Just twist your wrist slightly to the left, and you'll find that the fingers fall onto the right fret more comfortably.

Once you've practiced some changes from and to these new chords, go over the accompaniment using just the pattern in the first bar. After that you can try all the variations I've put in to make a more interesting sound. Right, take it slowly, and don't forget to keep a steady beat . . .

Accompaniment 4/4 Swing Rhythm   ↓↑ = Strum down/up

Verse

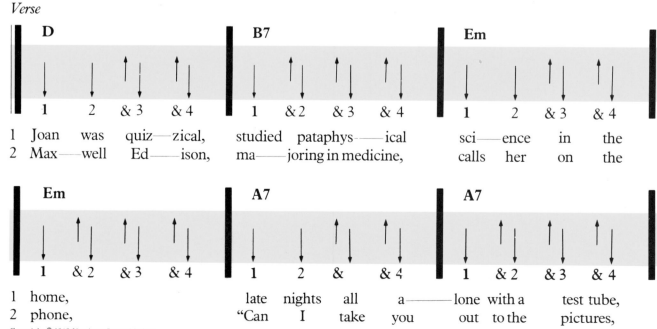

D

| 1 | 2 | & 3 | & 4 |

1 Joan was quiz—zical,
2 Max—well Ed—ison,

B7

| 1 | & 2 | & 3 | & 4 |

studied pataphys——ical
ma——joring in medicine,

Em

| 1 | 2 | & 3 | & 4 |

sci—ence in the
calls her on the

Em

| 1 | & 2 | & 3 | & 4 |

1 home,
2 phone,

A7

| 1 | 2 | & | & 4 |

late nights all a——lone with a
"Can I take you out to the

A7

| 1 | & 2 | & 3 | & 4 |

test tube,
pictures,

Maxwell's Silver Hammer Continued

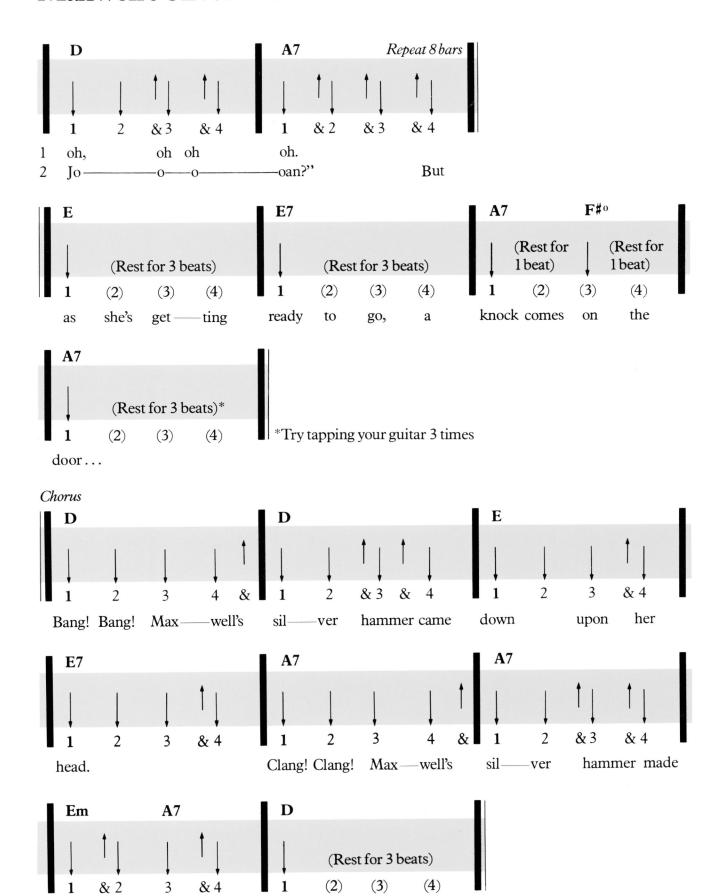

D

1 2 & 3 & 4

1 oh,   oh oh   oh.
2 Jo————o——o————————oan?"   But

E

(Rest for 3 beats)

1 (2) (3) (4)

as she's get——ting

E7

(Rest for 3 beats)

1 (2) (3) (4)

ready to go, a

A7   **F#°**

(Rest for   (Rest for
1 beat)   1 beat)

1 (2) (3) (4)

knock comes on the

A7

(Rest for 3 beats)*

1 (2) (3) (4)

door . . .

*Try tapping your guitar 3 times

Chorus

D

1 2 3 4 &

Bang! Bang! Max——well's

D

1 2 & 3 & 4

sil——ver hammer came

E

1 2 3 & 4

down   upon her

E7

1 2 3 & 4

head.

A7

1 2 3 4 &

Clang! Clang! Max——well's

A7

1 2 & 3 & 4

sil——ver hammer made

Em   **A7**

1 & 2 3 & 4

sure that she was

D

(Rest for 3 beats)

1 (2) (3) (4)

dead.

9

Ob-la-di Ob-la-da   Lennon/McCartney

Although the pattern stays the same all the way through this final strummer, it's not as easy as it seems – take care to change your left hand chord positions **on the upstroke** at the end of the bar, not on the last downstroke of the bar. Because the tempo must be quite fast, you certainly won't have time to leave the change until after the upstroke, but a muffled sound is perfectly O.K. when doing this kind of change. Take it slowly to begin with, as always.

Accompaniment 4/4 Rhythm   ↓↑ = Strum down/up

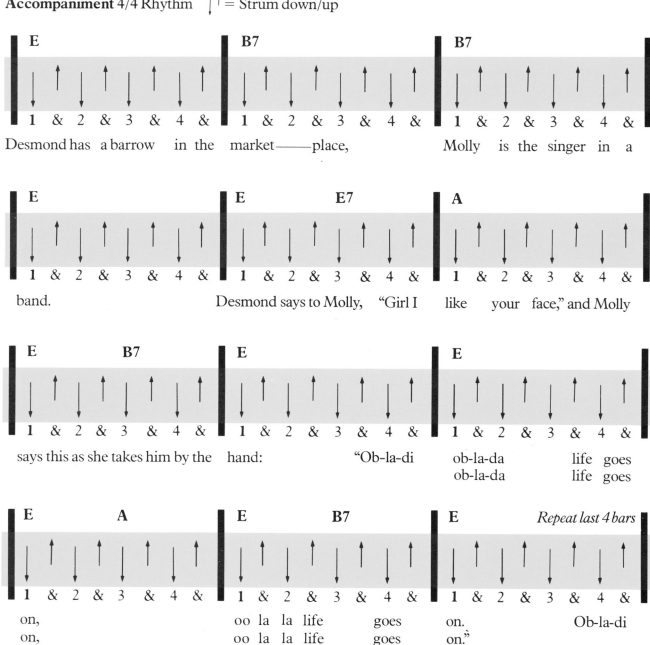

E		
1 & 2 & 3 & 4 &	1 & 2 & 3 & 4 &	1 & 2 & 3 & 4 &

Desmond has a barrow in the market——place,   Molly is the singer in a

band.   Desmond says to Molly, "Girl I like your face," and Molly

says this as she takes him by the hand: "Ob-la-di   ob-la-da   life goes
                                                        ob-la-da   life goes

on,   oo la la life   goes   on.   Ob-la-di
on,   oo la la life   goes   on."

Some New Ideas

Bass Runs

In the bass-strum style, the bass run is very important for breaking up the usual patterns. This kind of run usually goes from one chord to another, replacing one or more strums. Let's have a look at the most common bass run, and we'll use two very familiar chords to illustrate it...

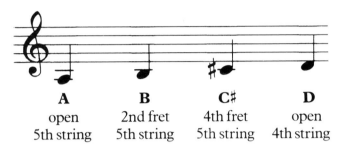

A	B	C♯	D
open	2nd fret	4th fret	open
5th string	5th string	5th string	4th string

Do you remember the notes on the treble clef? Good. The first note is **A** and, as I've shown, you can play it with the open 5th string. Using your first finger, play the 2nd fret, 5th string after that, and then with your third finger, play the 4th fret, 5th string. Finally play the open 4th string. (All these notes should be hit with the thumb of the right hand.) So you've played **A**, **B**, **C♯** and **D**. Do that sequence a few times till you're familiar with it.

How do you put this run into the bass-strum patterns? Well, this is one possible way...

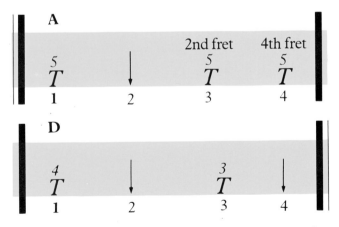

So you start off with the usual bass and downstroke, then put in the **B** note (with your first finger) and the **C♯** note (with your third finger). The run is completed on the first beat of the second bar, with the usual **D** note, open 4th string. That bar is finished off in the usual way. Try it very slowly, keeping a steady beat, and then speed up a bit.

Hammer-Ons

'Hammer-ons' are embellishments done with the left hand, after the right has struck a string. So two notes are produced with just one strike by the right hand. Because this effect is less difficult on the bass strings, let's try a couple on the 4th and 5th strings...

Use your first finger for the **D** to **E** hammer-on. So the right-hand thumb plays the open 4th string, and the first finger comes down firmly onto the 2nd fret (to produce an **E** note). Remember your music theory, you should count the two notes 1&, because they're eighth notes. Let the first note ring but then come down fast and hard, otherwise you'll deaden the string instead of producing another loud, clear note. After a few practices you'll get it better. The second one is similar, except on the 5th string – play the open-5th **A** and come down, with your second finger this time, on the 2nd fret for the **B** note.

Now try fingering a whole **A** chord and do the same on the 4th string, then a whole **E** chord, and do the same on the 5th string – it means you just raise the finger and place it firmly down again. Are you confident about runs and hammer-ons now? Good, to the songs.... .

Me And Bobby McGee

Let's go over the arrangement you played for this song, and add some hammer-ons and a bass run, like those you've just learned. First of all, try the **A** and **E** chord hammer-ons – they can fit into the patterns like this . . .

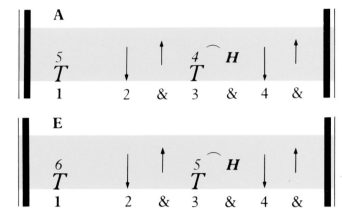

You could also try a hammer-on when playing the **D** chord. Raise your first finger and play the open string with your right hand, and put it firmly back again in the usual way. The open 3rd string is a **G** note, and the 2nd fret, 3rd string is an **A** note. See if you can work out how the bar should look and sound.

Now for a bass run. Going from the verse to the chorus will be very distinctive with a bass run. So instead of the bar you've been playing, try this one . . .

This bar isn't quite the same as the one on the previous page, but it's not hard. In fact, you don't even have to finger an **A** chord!

The Times They Are A-Changin'

When you stay on the same chord for two bars in a row, it's often a good idea to vary the second bar a little. One way to do this is to use a hammer-on. In this Dylan song, the second **D** bars and **A7** bars can look like this . . .

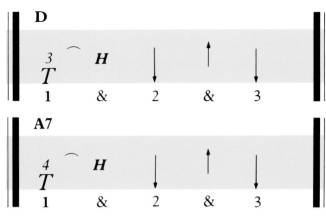

The second **A7** bar, toward the end of the verse, can be changed to a run . . .

The second **A7** bar, toward the end of the verse, can be changed to a run . . .

Colours

In the 4/4 rhythm patterns, it's often a good idea to use a hammer-on on the third beat, like this for the **D** and **A7** chord patterns . . .

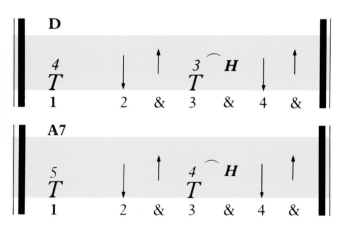

You could also put in a bass run from the **A7** to **D** (like the example on the previous page) right at the end of the accompaniment before starting another verse.

Drunken Sailor   Traditional, arranged Russ Shipton

This popular song is great for everybody to practice their sailor accents and make as much noise as possible! Before you try this accompaniment, you've got to learn two new chords, **D** minor and **C**. Try some left hand changes from one to the other, and then you'll be ready to have a go at the hammer-ons – they're similar to what you did on the **A** and **E** chords, so just raise your second finger in both cases, and put it back firmly again. You should get a clear note with no buzzing, played exactly halfway between the beats. Count the bars **1**, **2**, **3** & **4**.

I've sneaked a different kind of run ('chromatic', one fret at a time) into the accompaniment to give you a challenge – use your first finger for the 1st fret, **E♭** note. Good luck . . .

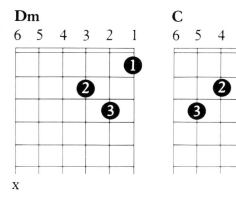

Accompaniment 4/4 Rhythm   ↓ = Strum down $\overset{3 \frown H}{T}$ = Thumb plays 3rd string, left hand
                 V = Verse   *C* = Chorus   hammers on

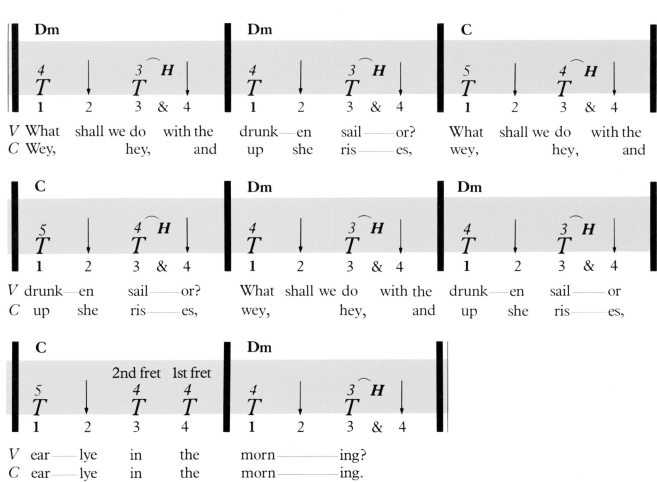

V What shall we do with the drunk—en sail——or? What shall we do with the
C Wey,   hey,   and up   she   ris——es,   wey,   hey,   and

V drunk—en sail——or?   What shall we do with the drunk—en sail——or
C up   she ris——es,   wey,   hey,   and   up   she   ris——es,

V ear——lye in the morn————ing?
C ear——lye in the morn————ing.

This Land Is Your Land

One Pattern First

Practice the hammer-on on the 5th string when fingering a **G** chord. Keep your second finger clear of the 5th string. When you can do that and the hammer-on on the 4th string in a **C** chord, play just one pattern to accompany this well-known Woody Guthrie song, like this ...

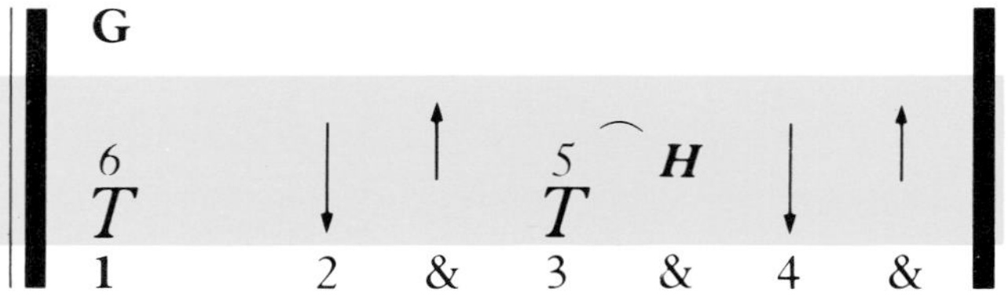

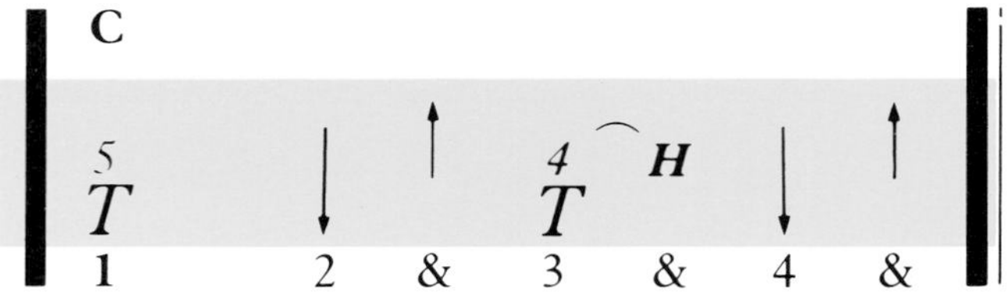

G

6 T	↓	↑	5 ⌒ T	H	↓	↑
1	2	&	3	&	4	&

C

5 T	↓	↑	4 ⌒ T	H	↓	↑
1	2	&	3	&	4	&

Once that comes easy, try doing the varied accompaniment on the next page, with the help of the notes below. If you want some more practice, add some upstrokes to the "Drunken Sailor" accompaniment, and try it again. It'll sound nice and full, but with upstrokes as well it'll be hard to get it as fast as it should be!

New Runs

First of all, let's have a look at the usual bass run from the **G** to **C** chord ... (this is very similar to the **A** to **D** run, just one tone lower)

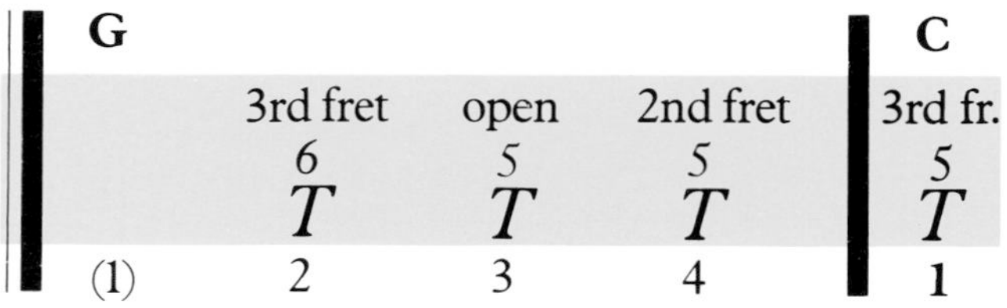

G .... **C**

	3rd fret	open	2nd fret	3rd fr.
	6 T	5 T	5 T	5 T
(1)	2	3	4	1

Play the 6th string **G** note, then take your hand off for the open 5th string. Put your first finger back for the **A** note, and finally play the **C** note when your left hand is in the full **C**-chord position.

The same notes are used in the accompaniment here, but you'll notice slight changes of timing – a

downstroke, for instance, is put in for the second beat. Count the bar in the usual way and you'll have no problems. Now have a look at a run from **D** to **G**

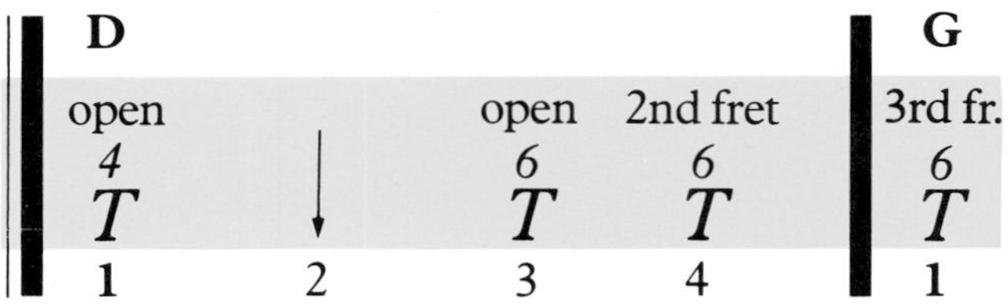

D .... **G**

open		open	2nd fret	3rd fr.
4 T	↓	6 T	6 T	6 T
1	2	3	4	1

For this run, play the downstroke on the second beat, then take your hand off and play the open 6th string. That's followed by the 2nd fret, 6th string, fingered by the **first** finger. The final note is of course **G** and you play that when you're back into a full **G** chord, on the 3rd fret of the 6th string.

Descending Runs

The two runs shown above are moving upward in pitch, but naturally you can go the other way, as we did in "Drunken Sailor." In the accompaniment on the next page, you'll find a descending run from **C** to **G**. The fingering is the same as the other way, using the first finger for the **B** note, and taking your left hand off to move into the **G**-chord position as you play the open 5th-string **A** note.

The Flatpick

Those of you who are using a steel string guitar (i.e. the two top treble strings are steel, not nylon) could try playing both the bass-strum and straight strumming styles with a flatpick. Persevere with a medium weight pick for a while, because anything new takes time to master, and soon you'll be able to graduate to bluegrass and rock 'n' roll.
Hold the pick between the thumb and the first finger, but have the thumb going **across** the finger. The pick is on the **side** of the first finger. This will give you a better grip, so you won't keep dropping the flatpick!

This Land Is Your Land   Woody Guthrie

Accompaniment 4/4 Rhythm   ↓↑ = Strum down/up $\overset{4\frown H}{T}$ = Thumb plays 4th string, left hand hammers on

Verse/Chorus

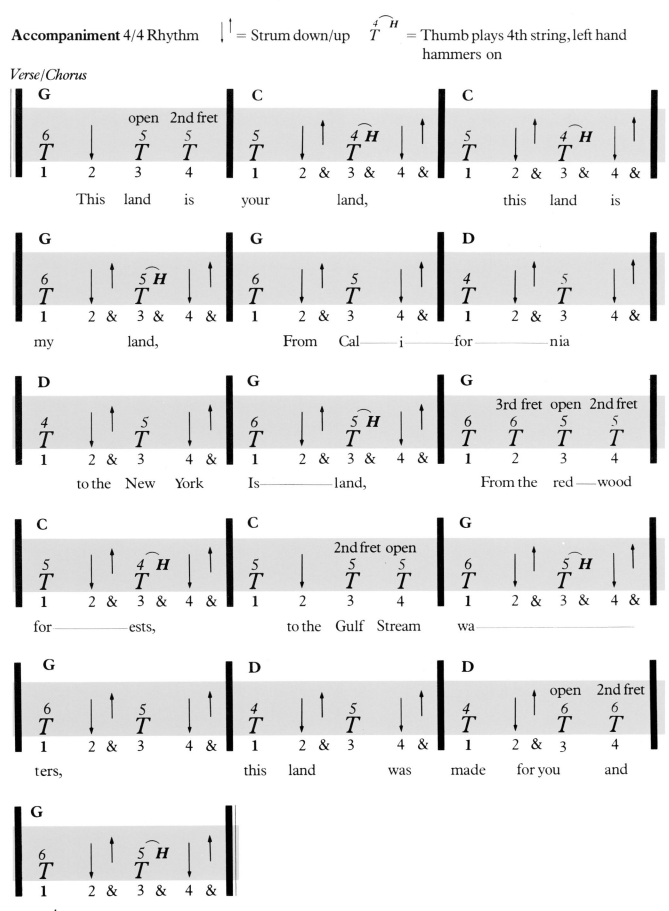

Summary

The Bass-Strum Style

Bass Runs

Bass runs are an extremely important method of linking chords, and making accompaniments sound more interesting, so let's run over some of the most common ones (most of which you've already used in some form) . . .

Usual Chords Involved	Notes	String and Fret
A to D	ABC♯D	5th open, 2nd, and 4th frets, 4th open
E to A	EF♯G♯A	6th open, 2nd, and 4th frets, 5th open
G to C	GABC	
D to G	DEF♯G	
Am to C	ABC	*
C to Dm	EE♭D	(reverse chromatic run)
C to G	CBAG	(reverse run)

*Can you find the right string and fret for the other runs?

I've given you the guitar positions for the first two runs, see if you can work out the others. The **C** to **Dm** run is a 'chromatic' one, meaning that the notes have only one semitone between them. What's similar about all the other runs? Yes, the intervals between the notes are **tone, tone, semitone** every time – except where a run is reversed, like the **C** to **G** one, (try reversing some of the others) or where you're going from a minor to a major or the other way.

Can you find any other bass runs?

Hammer-Ons

Let's look at hammer-ons in the same way. . .

Usual Chords Involved	Notes	
A, Am, A7, or C	D to E	4th string
D or Dm	G to A	
G, E, Em, or E7	A to B	*

*Can you find the right string?

What could you use for a hammer-on when fingering a **B7** chord? And what is similar about the two notes involved in each case? Yes, they're a tone (two frets) apart – these are the most common hammer-ons, but sometimes there are opportunities for hammer-ons involving notes just one semitone apart. Can you find any in the chords you know?

16

Some New Ideas

A New Pattern

You learned quite a few patterns in the first book, but there is another very distinctive one that goes well with that Animals hit of yesteryear, "The House Of The Risin' Sun"...

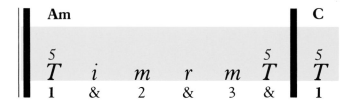

The last bass of the bar together with the first bass of the following bar make a kind of "short" bass run. This type of pattern stresses the first beat of each bar quite heavily.

Try this pattern with some other chords.

Bass Runs

Though the bass-strum style relies on the bass to provide the interest in the accompaniment, with hammers-on and bass runs, other styles can make good use of these embellishments. Here's the usual bass run from **A** to **D**, using the arpeggio style...

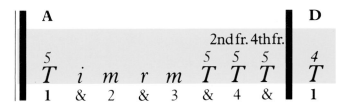

The first and third fingers are used for the **B** and **C** notes as before. The pattern doesn't have to be played fast, so the run can be done on the half beats.

Try some of the other runs you know using the arpeggio style.

Hammer-Ons

Hammer-ons used in the arpeggio style are often squeezed into a half beat, so instead of counting the beat as 1&, three notes come into one beat, and are counted 1&&. The note following the hammer-on comes in its usual place, exactly on the half beat, so the hammer-on is done quickly. You could say "da-da dar" to get the rhythm right. Try this hammer-on in an **Em** bar...

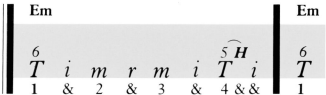

Now try hammer-ons with other chords and other arpeggio patterns that you know – both "fast" ones like above, and the slower ones that take up one-half beat.

Music Notation

So far I've used my simplified notation for all the accompaniments you've played. Though the strumming and bass-strum styles are much more easily written this way, the single-note styles can be shown in ordinary music notation without any trouble. Because it's **very** important that you know how to read at least the treble clef notes, "Sailing" is written in music notation. This will give you valuable practice in reading notes.

In the last section of this book there's a simple classical piece, and again it's written in ordinary music notation. That will give you practice in remembering the **length** of notes. Don't avoid working at these "academic" things, you'll find them very useful in time!

The House Of The Risin' Sun

Traditional, arranged Russ Shipton

This song has been around for a long time. The Animals had a hit with it in the sixties, and it's still played today. The chord sequence is more interesting than a lot of popular songs, but there's a new chord for you to learn – the **F** chord. You'll need more practice on this one than on the others so far, because it involves a 'barre.' That means a left-hand finger (almost always the first) must press down more than one string at a time . . .

Let your thumb drop slightly on the back of the neck, and push your wrist forward – but not too much, otherwise you'll lose your grip! You must adjust your arm and body position too, especially when using this shape at the end of the neck, without a capo. Try this accompaniment first with a **capo on the 4th fret.**

When you're happy with the **F** chord and can change from and to it, have a go at the bass run from **Am** to **C.** You play the **A, B,** and **C** notes for this run, and the **B** note is played with the second finger on the left hand. Raise this finger only – leave the first and third fingers in position, and then when you move to the **C**-chord position the third finger can come off the third string and go to the fifth string. But the first finger **stays** in its original position, so you don't have to move it.

All the other bass movements don't need left-hand finger changes, but watch carefully for any changes I've made on the bass notes.

F

F
6 5 4 3 2 1
① ① | Frets
| 1st
② | 2nd
③④ | 3rd
| 4th
| 5th

Accompaniment 3/4 Rhythm *T i m r* = Thumb, index, middle, and ring fingers

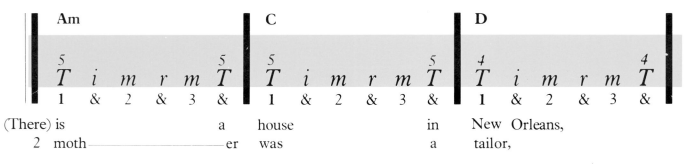

Am						C						D					
5				5		5				5		4					4
T	i	m	r	m	T	T	i	m	r	m	T	T	i	m	r	m	T
1	&	2	&	3	&	1	&	2	&	3	&	1	&	2	&	3	&

(There) is   a house   in New Orleans,

2 moth————er was   a tailor,

18

The House Of The Risin' Sun   Continued

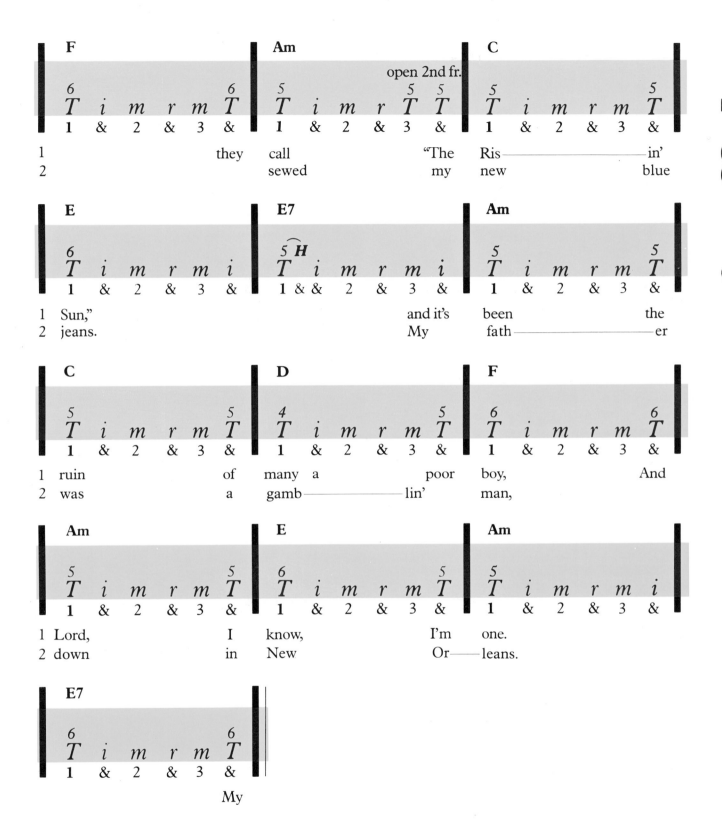

F

6				6	
T	*i*	*m*	*r*	*m*	*T*
1	&	2	&	3	&

1

2

           they   call

           sewed

Am

open 2nd fr.

5				5	5
T	*i*	*m*	*r*	*T*	*T*
1	&	2	&	3	&

1   "The

2   my

C

5					5
T	*i*	*m*	*r*	*m*	*T*
1	&	2	&	3	&

1 Ris————————in'

2 new————————blue

E

6					
T	*i*	*m*	*r*	*m*	*i*
1	&	2	&	3	&

1 Sun,"

2 jeans.

E7

5 $\frown$ **H**					
T	*i*	*m*	*r*	*m*	*i*
1 &&	2	&	3	&

        and it's

        My

Am

5					5
T	*i*	*m*	*r*	*m*	*T*
1	&	2	&	3	&

been————————the

fath————————er

C

5					5
T	*i*	*m*	*r*	*m*	*T*
1	&	2	&	3	&

1 ruin

2 was

D

4					5
T	*i*	*m*	*r*	*m*	*T*
1	&	2	&	3	&

of   many a   poor

a   gamb————lin'

F

6					6
T	*i*	*m*	*r*	*m*	*T*
1	&	2	&	3	&

boy,   And

man,

Am

5					5
T	*i*	*m*	*r*	*m*	*T*
1	&	2	&	3	&

1 Lord,

2 down

E

6					5
T	*i*	*m*	*r*	*m*	*T*
1	&	2	&	3	&

I   know,

in   New

Am

5					
T	*i*	*m*	*r*	*m*	*i*
1	&	2	&	3	&

I'm   one.

Or——leans.

E7

6					6
T	*i*	*m*	*r*	*m*	*T*
1	&	2	&	3	&

My

Sailing G. Sutherland

You'll all remember this one that was in the charts not long ago, sung by Rod Stewart. The chord sequence is quite interesting, and straightforward when the accompaniment is arranged in the key of G. One of the patterns you know forms the basis of the accompaniment, and I've added some bass runs and hammer-ons. Go over each bar very carefully before trying to play it and you won't have too much trouble mastering this arrangement.

Before you get down to it, have a look at this new chord; just one note is different from the **D** chord – which one is it?

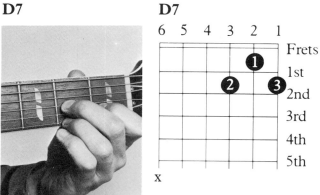

D7

6	5	4	3	2	1	
						Frets
				❶		1st
		❷			❸	2nd
						3rd
						4th
						5th

x

Accompaniment 4/4 Rhythm Standard music notation – see page 4.

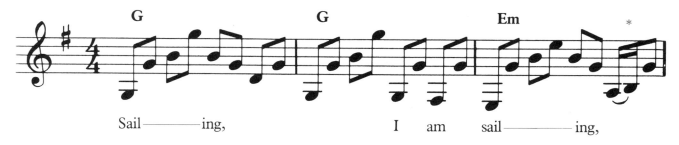

Sail———ing,   I   am   sail———ing,

* This sign means a hammer-on.
All 4th-, 5th-, and 6th-string notes are played with the right-hand thumb.

Sailing Continued

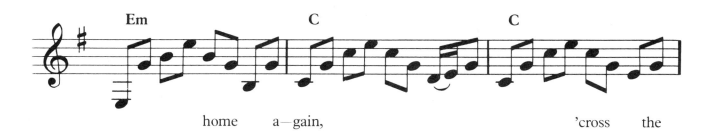

home   a—gain,   'cross   the

sea,   I   am   sail————ing

storm——y   wa|————ters,   to   be

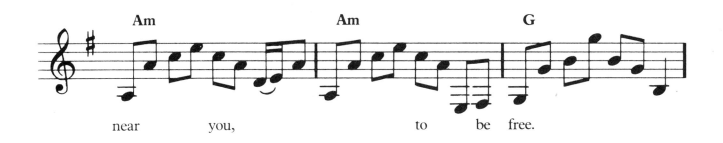

near   you,   to   be   free.

†Use your right-hand thumb and all three fingers
together.

How to Do It

Almost all modern and traditional acoustic guitarists use this style of playing – Paul McCartney, Steven Stills, Ralph McTell, John Denver, Donovan, Bob Dylan, and Gordon Lightfoot are just a few of the modern players who accompany their songs with the alternating thumb style. So obviously it's worth learning!

The essential ingredient of this style is naturally the alternating bass part – finger an **E** chord and try playing these notes with your right-hand thumb. Repeat the bar over and over again, keeping a very steady rhythm . . .

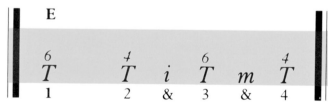

Don't move your right hand too much, or you'll not be able to hit exactly the right string each time. And keep your thumb just to the left of your fingers and they won't get in the way of each other.

While these bass notes give you a solid and interesting rhythm, some treble notes can be added to pick out the melody or harmonize with what you're singing, at the same time. **For now** let's stick with the usual chord shapes for the left hand, and use the trebles that we've got, to harmonize with the melody. Try this simple pattern, which involves just two treble notes. Count it carefully and play it slowly to begin with – do the same bar over and over again . . .

For the moment, **your index finger** on the right hand **will** *always play* **the 2nd string,** and the **middle finger will** *always play* **the 1st string.** Later we'll change these strict rules.

Are you happy with your control of the pattern now? Fine, see how you get on with another song you're sure to know, "Freight Train" . . .

Simple 4/4 Pattern Sequence (finger an **E** chord)

Thumb strikes 6th string

Thumb strikes 4th string

Index finger strikes 2nd string

Thumb strikes 6th string

Middle finger strikes 1st string

Thumb strikes 4th string

Freight Train James and Williams

In Book 4 I'll be giving you a much more complicated version of this accompaniment, where you'll pick out the melody notes and use more chords. For the moment, as with the other styles, we're using a very common pattern all the way through the first song. That way you'll get a good grounding in the alternating thumb style. The pattern is the one I showed on the previous page – don't forget to play slowly but steadily, using your index finger to play the 2nd string, and middle finger to play the 1st string . . .

Accompaniment 4/4 Rhythm $T i m$ = Thumb, index, and middle fingers

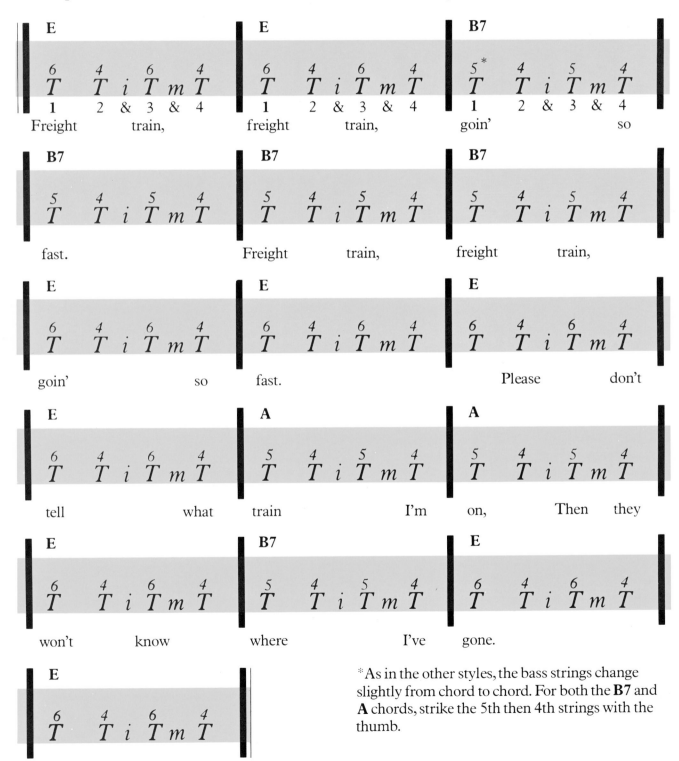

*As in the other styles, the bass strings change slightly from chord to chord. For both the **B7** and **A** chords, strike the 5th then 4th strings with the thumb.

If I Were A Carpenter   Tim Hardin

Tim Hardin wrote a number of beautiful songs in the sixties, but this is perhaps his best-known one, made a hit by Bobby Darin. The chords are straightforward, but the sequence is a bit unusual – normally in the key of D you wouldn't be playing a **C** chord.

So you can get the hang of this style more quickly, I've only made one change in the pattern that you used for "Freight Train"– instead of hitting the bass note on the first beat by itself, you're going to play the 1st string at the same time. That's called a 'pinch' because of the action of the thumb and finger together, and isn't hard. So the large *P* means you've got to play both the thumb on the string shown, together with the 1st string (played as usual with the middle finger on the right hand). Practice it with each of the chords a few times first, and away you go . . .

Accompaniment 4/4 Rhythm $\overset{4}{P}$ = Thumb plays 4th string and **middle finger plays 1st string**
i m = index and middle fingers
Verse

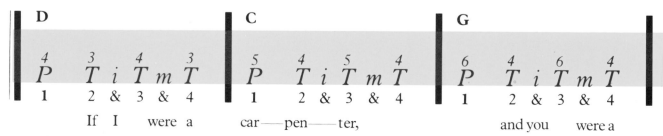

If I Were A Carpenter Continued

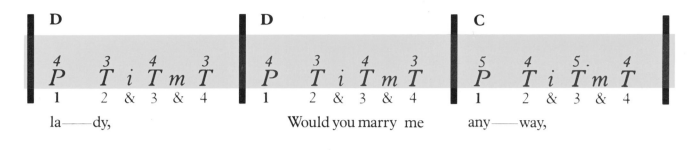

D		D		C	
4 3 4 3		4 3 4 3		5 4 5. 4	
P T i T m T		P T i T m T		P T i T m T	
1 2 & 3 & 4		1 2 & 3 & 4		1 2 & 3 & 4	
la——dy,		Would you marry me		any——way,	

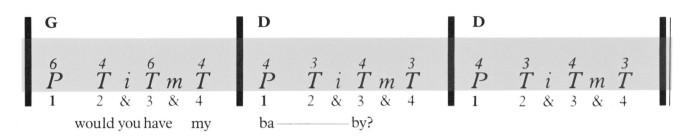

G		D		D	
6 4 6 4		4 3 4 3		4 3 4 3	
P T i T m T		P T i T m T		P T i T m T	
1 2 & 3 & 4		1 2 & 3 & 4		1 2 & 3 & 4	
would you have my		ba————by?			

Repeat these 9 bars for 2nd verse, then go to the chorus.

Chorus

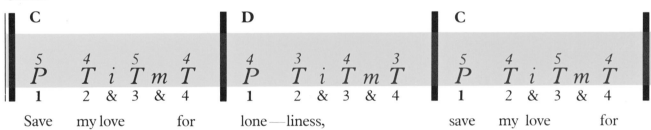

C		D		C	
5 4 5 4		4 3 4 3		5 4 5 4	
P T i T m T		P T i T m T		P T i T m T	
1 2 & 3 & 4		1 2 & 3 & 4		1 2 & 3 & 4	
Save my love for		lone—liness,		save my love for	

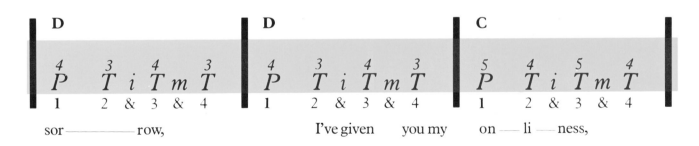

D		D		C	
4 3 4 3		4 3 4 3		5 4 5 4	
P T i T m T		P T i T m T		P T i T m T	
1 2 & 3 & 4		1 2 & 3 & 4		1 2 & 3 & 4	
sor————row,		I've given you my		on — li — ness,	

G		D		D	
6 4 6 4		4 3 4 3		4 3 4 3	
P T i T m T		P T i T m T		P T i T m T	
1 2 & 3 & 4		1 2 & 3 & 4		1 2 & 3 & 4	
give me your to——mor————row.					

More Ideas On The Alternating Thumb Style

Other Chords

Use the two patterns you know (one with thumb strikes on all four beats, the other with a pinch on the first beat) for all the chords you've learned so far. Here are the bass strings that are most commonly played with particular chords, though later other possibilities will be used in your accompaniments.

E Em E7 F G = 6th/4th strings (also try 6th/3rd)
A Am A7 B7 C = 5th/4th strings (also try 5th/3rd)
D Dm D7 = 4th/3rd strings (also try 4th/5th)

So you will play different bass notes with each chord but, for the moment, play the same top two treble strings with all of them. Play each chord and pattern over and over again, trying to build up speed but keeping the tempo steady. Once you're satisfied that you can play all of these smoothly, have a go at the different patterns below.

Other Patterns

Before you get on to Book 3, which has several variations on what you've done so far, try these two patterns (using different chords)...

T		T	m	T	i	T	
1		2	&	3	&	4	

T	i	T	m	T	i	T	m
1	&	2	&	3	&	4	&

The first one you'll probably recognize as the same as the first one you learned, with the two treble notes switched around. The other one is what I call a "continuous" pattern, because there are treble notes between each beat. If you don't change chords, you should be able to build up quite a bit of speed with this one.

When you've mastered these new patterns, and have got a nice bounce with your thumb, try changing chords and switching from one pattern to another.

Finally, I wonder if you can find one or more new patterns in the alternating thumb style yourself?

Other Songs

Some of the 4/4 songs that you've played from Book 1 are well suited to an alternating thumb accompaniment. Try re-arranging these songs in this style:

Blowin' In The Wind/ The Last Thing On My Mind/ Colours

'This Land Is Your Land' from this book could also be played with the alternating thumb style. Have a go at these more traditional ones as well...

Froggy Went A-Courtin'/Hard Traveling/ Oh Susannah/Midnight Special

How to Do It

In fact, there are many different ways of playing the guitar in a classical style, as there are in the other main areas of guitar music. But there are no obvious divisions like strumming, bass-strum, arpeggio, and alternating thumb in the folk music area.

Maybe then you could say that the difference between the classical and other styles of playing is that it is more random – it doesn't stick to patterns anywhere near as much as folk or modern guitar music. There is of course another very important difference – almost always classical music is instrumental. It isn't an accompaniment for a song.

When a piece is an instrumental, it's **extremely** important to get the notes clear and to give them their full time-value. It is of course very important to play all types of music well, but perhaps this classical 'study' on the next page (and others in Books 3 and 4) will help you to concentrate on making the most of what you're playing.

Have a look at the first bar – can you remember how long the notes should last? If you've been working out or checking parts of the song melodies so far, you should know the pitch of the notes on the treble clef too . . .

This means there are **4 beats** in each bar (i.e. 4 foot taps)

This means that the **length** of each beat is one quarter-note (or 4 quarter-notes in each bar)

Fingers

There are no hard and fast rules on which right-hand finger you should use, but when two notes come on the same string one after the other, it's often a good idea for smoothness to swap fingers. I'll indicate which finger I think you should use, above each note.

As for the left hand, classical players put down **only** the fingers they need at the time. With folk and modern music, players often use the whole chord shape. In fact, with classical music, the emphasis is not on chords at all.

The finger that you must use for each note in this piece will be the **same as the fret number** i.e. if the note is on the 1st fret, then you must use your **first** finger, if the note's on the 2nd fret, you use your second finger and so on. Only the first three frets are used in this one, so you'll only have to use your first three left-hand fingers.

Finding the Notes on the Guitar

As you've been doing when finding and playing the melody notes of the songs, look for the lowest position for each note. In fact, in this piece, the 3rd fret is the highest that you go, so they'll be quite easy to find!

In the classical style the thumb must be kept clear of the fingers

Study

Here is your first classical piece, a study by a composer and guitarist of the early nineteenth century. Take each bar separately and make sure you have the right frets for the notes. Persevere at reading the standard music notation, and you'll soon find it quite easy.

Try to make each note last as long as the music says it should last. Don't take your finger off as soon as you've played the note – it's often better to leave one finger where it is until the next has played. The sound can then be much smoother.

Study   Fernando Sor

Instrumental 4/4 Rhythm Standard music notation – see pages 4 and 27 *T m i* = thumb, middle, and index fingers, right hand

Section one

This sign means 'repeat'. In this case you go back to the start and play all 8 bars of Section one again.

Section two

repeat Section two

The Classical Style

The Major Scale

The C Major Scale

Before going on to Book 3, I'd like you to think about the Do Re Mi etc. that you've all sung at one time or another. It's the major scale that you're singing, but which one it is depends on which note is the starting note. All major scales sound similar in an overall way because the spaces or intervals between the notes are always the same. Let's have a look at the **C** major scale – that's the one where we don't have to bother with flats or sharps . . .

The **C** Major Scale

C   D   E   F   G   A   B   C

To play this scale on your guitar, start by putting your third finger of the left hand on the 3rd fret of the 5th string. Because guitar music is written an octave lower than it's played (as I said on page 4), this is where you play your starting note. Alternate the first two right-hand fingers (don't bother with the thumb for this exercise) and use the usual left-hand fingers on the appropriate frets.

When you've worked out where the notes are for the left hand, and you've played the **C** scale smoothly through a couple of times, see if you can work out which notes from this scale are used for the **C** chord (or **C** major chord, to give its full name). Also, what **are** the intervals between the notes of a major scale (which are always the same)? And what's the interval, in terms of both frets and tones, between the low **C** and high **C** notes?

Now see if you can write out the **G** major scale in the same way that I've written the **C** scale above. If you keep the intervals between the notes in the same order, you should find one note that has to be 'sharped' i.e. raised in pitch by a semitone, or fret. And then can you play it on the guitar?

Ask your teacher if you're not sure of these scales – they're pretty important, because the chords you've been playing come from scales. See if you can memorize the intervals of the major scale before the next book.

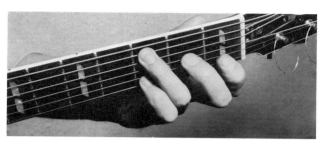

C note (low)
D note (open 4th string)

E note

F note
G note (open 3rd string)

A note
B note (open 2nd string)

C note (high)

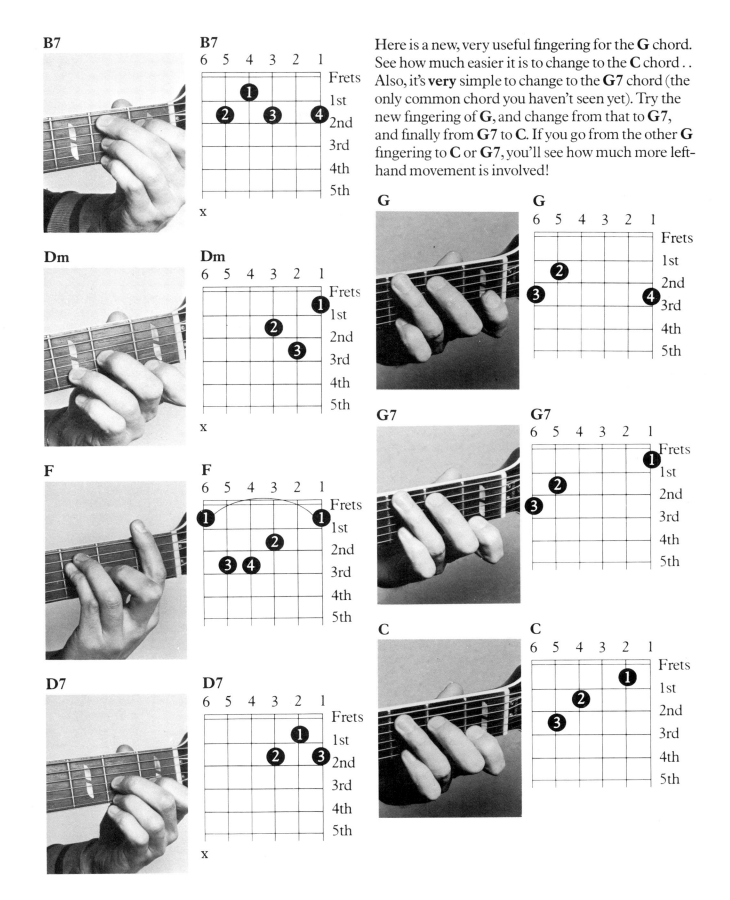

Here is a new, very useful fingering for the **G** chord. See how much easier it is to change to the **C** chord.. Also, it's **very** simple to change to the **G7** chord (the only common chord you haven't seen yet). Try the new fingering of **G**, and change from that to **G7**, and finally from **G7** to **C**. If you go from the other **G** fingering to **C** or **G7**, you'll see how much more left-hand movement is involved!

31

Lyrics

Yellow Submarine

Verse 1:
In the town where I was born, lived a man who sailed to sea,
And he told us of his life in the land of submarines.
Chorus:
We all live in a yellow submarine, yellow submarine, yellow submarine.
We all live in a yellow submarine, yellow submarine, yellow submarine.
Verse 2:
So we sailed up to the sun, till we found the sea of green,
And we lived beneath the waves, in our yellow submarine.
Verse 3:
And our friends are all on board, many more of them live next door
And the band begins to play...
Verse 4:
As we live a life of ease, everyone of us has all we need
Sky of blue, sea of green, in our yellow submarine.

Maxwell's Silver Hammer

Verse 1:
Joan was quizzical, studied pat-a-physical science in the home,
Late nights all alone with a test tube, oh, oh oh oh.
Maxwell Edison, majoring in medicine, calls her on the phone,
"Can I take you out to the pictures Jo - o - o - oan?"
But as she's getting ready to go, a knock comes on the door.
Chorus:
Bang! Bang! Maxwell's silver hammer came down upon her head.
Clang! Clang! Maxwell's silver hammer made sure that she was dead.
Verse 2:
Back in school again, Maxwell plays the fool again, teacher gets annoyed,
Wishing to avoid an unpleasant sce - e - e - ene.
She tells Max to stay when the class has gone away so he waits behind
Writing fifty times "I must not be so - o - o - o."
But when she turns her back on the boy, he creeps up from behind...
Verse 3:
P.C. Thirty-One said, "We've caught a dirty one,"
Maxwell stands alone
Painting testimonial pictures, oh, oh oh oh.

Rose and Valerie, screaming from the gallery, say, "He must go free."
The judge does not agree and he tells them so - o - o - o.
But as the words are leaving his lips, a noise comes from behind...

Ob-la-di Ob-la-da

Verse 1:
Desmond has a barrow in the market place,
Molly is the singer in a band.
Desmond says to Molly, "Girl I like your face,"
And Molly says this as she takes him by the hand:
Chorus:
Ob-la-di ob-la-da life goes on, oo, la la
life goes on *(rpt)*.
Middle Section:
In a couple of years they have built a home sweet home.
With a couple of kids running in the yard of Desmond and Molly Jones.
Verse 2:
Desmond takes a trolley to the jeweller's store, buys a twenty carat golden ring,
Takes it back to Molly waiting at the door, and as he gives it to her she begins to sing:
Verse 3:
Happy ever after in the marketplace, Desmond lets the children lend a hand
Molly stays at home and does her pretty face and in the evening she still sings it with the band:

Drunken Sailor

Verse 1:
What shall we do with the drunken sailor?
What shall we do with the drunken sailor?
What shall we do with the drunken sailor
Earlye in the morning?
Chorus:
Wey, hey, and up she rises,
Wey, hey, and up she rises,
Wey, hey, and up she rises,
Earlye in the morning.

32

Verse 2:
Put him in the scuppers with a hose-pipe on him *(3x)*
Earlye in the morning.
Verse 3:
Put him in the longboat until he's sober *(3 x)*
Earlye in the morning.
Verse 4:
Tie him by the legs in a running bowline *(3x)*
Earlye in the morning.

This Land Is Your Land

Verse/Chorus:
This land is your land, this land is my land,
From California to the New York island,
From the redwood forests to the Gulf Stream waters,
This land was made for you and me!
Verse 2:
As I went walking that ribbon of highway
I saw above me that endless skyway.
I saw below me that golden valley,
This land was made for you and me!
Verse 3:
I roamed and rambled and I followed my footsteps
To the sparkling sands of her diamond deserts
And all around me a voice was sounding.
This land was made for you and me!
Verse 4:
When the sun came shining, then I was strolling
And the wheat fields waving, and the dust clouds rolling.
A voice was chanting, as the fog was lifting.
This land was made for you and me!

The House Of The Risin' Sun

Verse 1:
There is a house in New Orleans, they call "The Risin' Sun."
And it's been the ruin of many a poor boy,
And Lord, I know, I'm one.
Verse 2:
My mother was a tailor, sewed my new blue jeans.
My father was a gamblin' man, down in New Orleans.
Verse 3:
Now the only thing to gamblin' is a suitcase and a trunk

And the only time he's satisfied is when he's on a drunk.
Verse 4:
Go tell my baby sister not to do what I have done
To shun that house in New Orleans, they call "The Risin' Sun."
Verse 5:
One foot on the platform, the other's on the train.
I'm goin' back to New Orleans, to wear that ball and chain.

Sailing

Verse 1:
Sailing, I am sailing, home again, 'cross the sea,
I am sailing, stormy waters, to be near you, to be free.
Verse 2:
I am flying, I am flying, like a bird, 'cross the sky,
I am flying, passing high clouds, to be with you, to be free.
Verse 3:
Can you hear me? Can you hear me? Through the dark night, far away.
I am dying, forever trying, to be with you, who can say?

Freight Train

Verse/Chorus:
Freight train, freight train, goin' so fast.
Freight train, freight train, goin' so fast.
Please don't tell what train I'm on,
Then they won't know where I've gone.
Verse 2:
When I'm dead and in my grave
No more good times will I crave.
Place the stones at my head and feet
And tell them that I've gone to sleep.
Verse 3:
When I die, Lord, bury me deep,
Way down on old Chestnut Street,
So I can hear old number nine
As she comes rollin' by.
Verse 4:
When I die, Lord, bury me deep,
Way down on old Chestnut Street.
Place the stones at my head and feet
And tell them that I'm still asleep.

33

If I Were A Carpenter

Verse 1:
If I were a carpenter, and you were a lady,
Would you marry me anyway, would you have my baby?
Chorus:
Save my love for loneliness, save my love for sorrow,
I've given you my onliness, give me your tomorrow.
Verse 2:
If a tinker were my trade, would you still find me?
Carrying the pots I made, following behind me?
Verse 3:
If I were a miller, at my mill wheel grinding,
Would you miss your colored blouse, and your soft shoes shining?
Verse 4:
If I worked my hands in wood, would you still love me?
Answer me, babe, "Yes I would, I'd place you above me."

Playing

Well done! You've persevered through to the end of the second book. There are more advanced things coming up in the next two books, but if you've understood everything in the first two books, you won't have too much trouble carrying on the good work. If you're still making buzzing noises with your left hand instead of producing clear notes, now's the time to tighten up your loose fingering. Once you get used to fingering firmly and accurately, it's quite easy to do.

If you're finding it particularly difficult to press down the strings, check for correct 'action'. The height of the strings should be right – i.e. they shouldn't have to be pressed down a long way.

Singing

Two things are particularly important for your singing. Firstly, the pitch of the melody notes shouldn't be out of your vocal range. In class, some people won't like the key that the teacher has chosen, while others will find it just right. It doesn't matter too much in class, and everyone can't be completely satisfied, but you can experiment at home with the capo position in order to match your voice. Secondly, try to breathe in the natural pauses of a song, i.e. at the end of a line. If the song is fast, you may get away with waiting till after the second line. Don't breathe just anywhere, or the song won't sound very smoothly performed at all.

Songs

It's always a great feeling to discover things yourself, and to do your own arranging. You've got plenty of styles and patterns to try out on any new songs you get hold of.

Listening

Always **listen** to your own playing as well as that of others. The first step is listening carefully to the notes as you tune up your guitar each day. Then listen to the sounds you're actually making when you're playing the songs you know. Finally, listen to those around you, and of course the professional guitarists on record and live. See if you can recognize any of the styles you've learned so far! See you in the next book . . .

The Complete Guitar Player

by Russ Shipton.

Songs and music in this book
Call And Answer
Goin' Places
Jamaica Farewell
Michael Row The Boat Ashore
Moon Shadow
Morning Has Broken
Passing Note Waltz
She'll Be Coming Round The Mountain
Streets Of London
Study: Fernando Carulli
Suzanne
Take Me Home Country Roads
This Train
Where Have All The Flowers Gone?

Amsco Publications New York/London/Sydney/Cologne

Scales

Did you try that bit of homework I gave you at the end of Book 2? Well, if you found it difficult, you'll find the answers to my questions on this page. In a sense, most western music is bound up with the idea of the major scale, so the Do Re Mi Fa So La Ti Do that you've known for some time is more important than you may have thought!

What Is a Scale?

A scale is a series of notes that starts and ends with a note of the same name (but an octave higher). There are various scales, but the major scale, with eight notes and intervals of tone, tone, semitone, tone, tone, tone, semitone, is the one which is most important . . .

The C Major Scale

	C	D	E	F	G	A	B	C
Intervals . . .	⌊t⌋	⌊t⌋	⌊st⌋	⌊t⌋	⌊t⌋	⌊t⌋	⌊st⌋	

t = tone   st = semitone

The Scale and the Melody

You may be wondering what the connection is between the major scale and the songs and accompaniments that you've been singing and playing. Well, when playing in the key of C, for example (that usually means starting and ending with a **C** chord), it means that all the melody notes and probably the accompanying notes as well, will **normally** be from the major scale of the key note, in this case the C major scale.

The Scale and Bass Runs

You may have noticed that the common bass runs used in Book 2 are part of the scale. The last half of the scale of C is the run you used from the **G** chord to the **C** chord: **G, A, B,** and **C** to finish.

Other Major Scales

Because some chords are a lot easier to finger than others, most guitarists (particularly modern players) will play in the keys of C, G, D, A, and E (or they might use a capo). The key of C, as you see above, has no sharp or flat notes. The others involve one or more notes being sharped, in order to produce the same intervals between the notes. Let's have a look at the G major scale . . .

The G Major Scale* (**F** is sharp)

G A B C D E F♯ G
⌊t⌋⌊t⌋⌊st⌋⌊t⌋⌊t⌋⌊t⌋⌊st⌋

If you examine the gaps or intervals between the notes, only the **F** note must be altered. By making it an **F♯**, there is a tone from the **E** note, and a semitone to the **G** note, as required.

Now try the D major scale* (**F** and **C** are sharp)

D E F♯ G A B C♯ D
⌊t⌋⌊t⌋⌊st⌋⌊t⌋⌊t⌋⌊t⌋⌊st⌋

As with the G scale, we have to check the gaps between the notes. They should always be tone, tone, semitone, tone, tone, tone, semitone. So the **F** and **C** notes must both be sharped.

Now see if you work out the notes in the A and E major scales. All you have to do is to keep the same intervals that the major scale must always have, and flat or sharp any notes where necessary.

On the next page we'll look at the relationship of the major scale and chords, but before moving on, practice playing these five scales at the lower end of the fingerboard, and try to remember the notes as you play them.

*The sharp signs (♯) at the beginning of a stave, tell you that all those notes, high or low, are always played sharp.

Chords

Now you've got the idea of the major scale, on this page we'll see how the chords you've been using are related to it.

What's a Chord?

I asked this question before, on page 10 of Book 1, but because chords are very important, we need to look at them more closely. A chord is three or more notes played together. These notes are found in the major scale of the key that the melody is in, and are either the same as the melody note, or harmonize with it.

The chords that you've learned so far have notes that are always certain intervals apart – intervals that are most natural or pleasing to the ear.

Where Do Chords Come From?

In any particular key, the chords you'd expect to find in an accompaniment come from the major scale of the key or 'tonic' note. Three very important chords are those with their root notes (the note that gives the chord its name) in the first, fourth, and fifth positions of the scale . . .

The C Major Scale

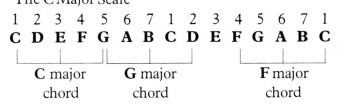

A common chord consists of three notes: the root note, plus the note two steps above it, plus the note two steps above that one. So the **C** chord (**C** major chord, in full) has the **C**, **E**, and **G** notes in it, while the **F** and **G** chords have **F**, **A**, and **C**, and **G**, **B**, and **D** notes respectively. One important alternative to the **G** chord is the **G7** chord. This has four notes in it: the **G**, **B** and **D** of the **G** chord plus the **F** note.

Apart from the three most important chords shown for the C major scale, what other chords might you expect in an accompaniment? Well, any of the chords that have their root notes in the other positions of the scale. So, returning to the scale, let's see what chords emerge, if we take two other notes and the root note in the same way as above . . .

The C Major Scale

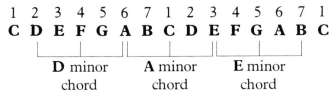

So there are three major chords, **C**, **F**, and **G**, plus three minor chords, **D**, **E**, and **A**. One more chord, the **B** diminished, would be produced from the **B** (the root note), **D**, and **F**, but this diminished chord isn't used as much as the others.

Other Keys

Just as the major scale intervals stay the same, so do the types of chords. Let's have a look at the G major scale, and what chords to expect when a song is in the key of G . . .

The G Major Scale

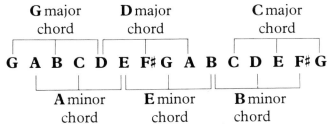

See if you can do the same thing for the keys of D, A, and E.

Moon Shadow Cat Stevens

Melody Notes

All of the melody notes of "Moon Shadow" (apart from the middle section, see page 7) are from the D major scale: **D E F♯ G A B C♯ D** etc. If you have a copy of **The Complete Guitar Player Songbook,** you can see this quite clearly.

Chords

The chords that you'd most expect in the key of D are the three used in the simpler arrangement – **D** major, **G** major, and **A** major. The other chords that you might also expect come into the more difficult, alternative arrangement.
Try the simpler arrangement first, and then substitute the chords in brackets for those next to them. You don't know the **B** minor and **F♯** minor chords, so have a look at them now . . .

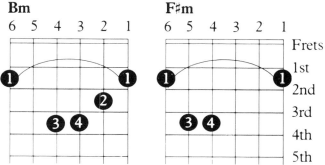

These are barre chords, and not too easy, so practice some chord changes to and from them with just the left hand. Then try the more difficult arrangement.

So that you'll fully understand the information on the last two pages, let's examine our first song in this book with the major scale in mind. This arrangement of the famous Cat Stevens song is in the key of D.

Accompaniment 4/4 Rhythm　↓↑ = Strum down/up　⌢**H** =hammer-on　*i* =index finger

Chorus

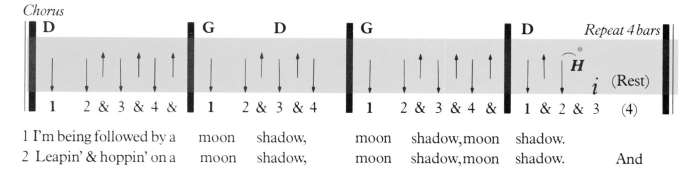

1 I'm being followed by a　moon　shadow,　moon　shadow, moon　shadow.
2 Leapin' & hoppin' on a　moon　shadow,　moon　shadow, moon　shadow.　　And

*Take your second finger off for the downstrum, and put it back down firmly for the hammer-on. Then strike the second string with your index finger.

Moon Shadow Continued

Verse

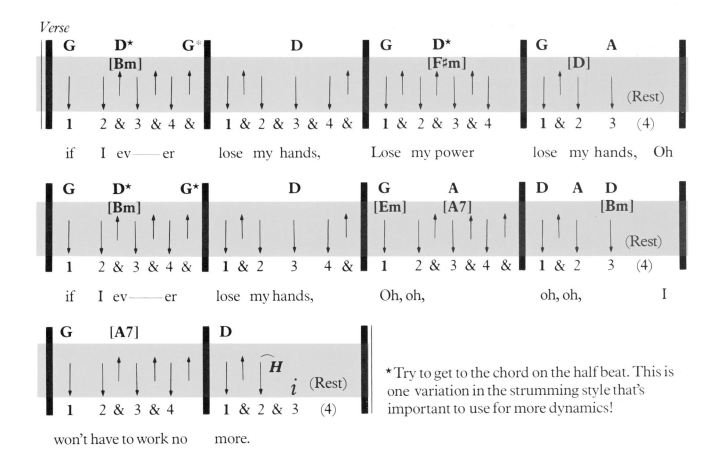

G **D★** **G***	**D**	**G** **D★**	**G** **A**
[Bm]		[F#m]	[D] (Rest)
1 2 & 3 & 4 &	1 & 2 & 3 & 4 &	1 & 2 & 3 & 4	1 & 2 3 (4)
if I ev——er	lose my hands,	Lose my power	lose my hands, Oh

G **D★** **G***	**D**	**G** **A**	**D** **A** **D**
[Bm]		[Em] [A7]	[Bm] (Rest)
1 2 & 3 & 4 &	1 & 2 3 4 &	1 2 & 3 & 4 &	1 & 2 3 (4)
if I ev——er	lose my hands,	Oh, oh,	oh, oh, I

G [A7]	**D**
	H i (Rest)
1 2 & 3 & 4	1 & 2 & 3 (4)
won't have to work no	more.

★Try to get to the chord on the half beat. This is one variation in the strumming style that's important to use for more dynamics!

Key Change

Normally the notes of a melody come only from the major scale of the key, but sometimes 'accidental' notes come into the melody line. Apart from accidentals, there's another important reason for other nonscale notes to come into the tune – a key change. Often the key change lasts for just a few bars, as in Moon Shadow, but sometimes the composer is more ambitious and the key change is one that lasts for some time. The key changes here to the key of **A**, and you'll notice the **G#** note in the melody of this section. Then it's back to **D** for the chorus.

Middle Section

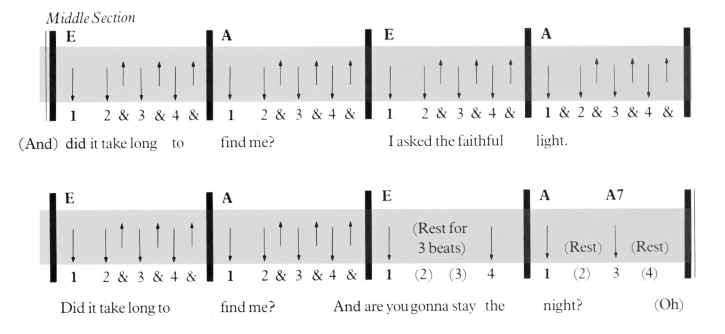

E	**A**	**E**	**A**
1 2 & 3 & 4 &	1 2 & 3 & 4 &	1 2 & 3 & 4 &	1 & 2 & 3 & 4 &
(And) did it take long to	find me?	I asked the faithful	light.

E	**A**	**E**	**A** **A7**
		(Rest for 3 beats)	(Rest) (Rest)
1 2 & 3 & 4 &	1 2 & 3 & 4 &	1 (2) (3) 4	1 (2) 3 (4)
Did it take long to	find me?	And are you gonna stay the	night? (Oh)

Jamaica Farewell   Traditional, arranged Russ Shipton

It's off to the Caribbean for some calypso rhythm! If you thought there was nothing more to strumming, you're wrong – 'syncopation' is a very important aspect of interesting strumming, and the pattern used for this song will certainly give you a lead-in to offbeat techniques. Taking a strong bass or downstroke and putting it between the beats gives the rhythm a very different flavor.

Straighten out your fingers on the first strum, and follow through with your thumb (use the flesh part). That's the "1&". Then do an up/down strum with the fingers, followed by another thumb strum, and three more finger strums to end the pattern. Both the finger and thumb strums should be smooth and flowing – glide across the strings. Each strum must follow evenly after the last – give the same amount of time to each strum and you'll soon get that lovely, jumping calypso rhythm.

Any offbeat rhythm is **very** hard to sing with, so make sure you can play the accompaniment well before attempting to sing at the same time!

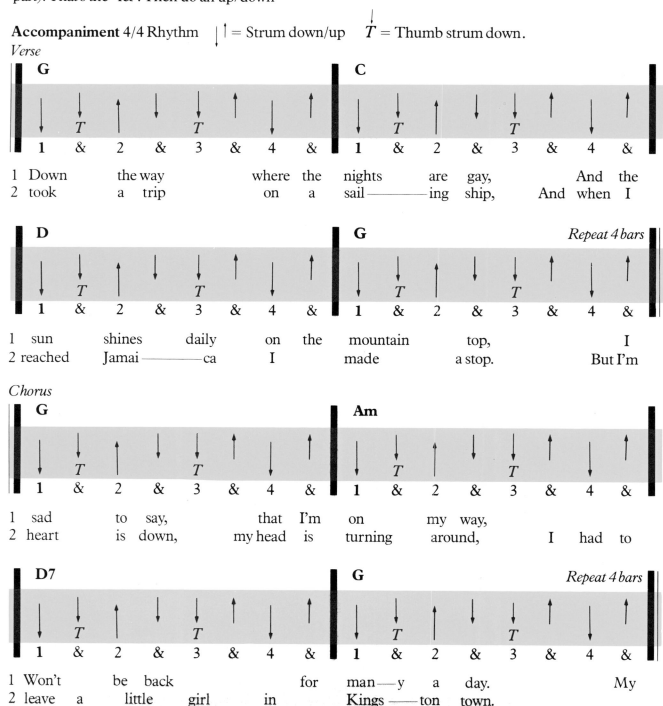

Accompaniment 4/4 Rhythm   ↓↑ = Strum down/up   *T* = Thumb strum down.

Transposing

You've probably found that "Jamaica Farewell" in the key of G is too high (or low) for your voice. Instead of using your capo, as you've done so far, read the information below and then try to change the key of the song (and others that you've had difficulty with) **without using a capo.**

Using a Capo

'Transposing' means adjusting music up or down in pitch. The melody notes change and the chords, of course, change with them by an equal amount. It's quite easy because music is a system of patterns. When you play and sing in the key of G, for example, and then put your capo on the 2nd fret but keep the same chord shapes, you're actually playing in the key of A, one tone higher. No new chord shapes have to be worked out and your voice automatically adjusts to the new key. And you don't have to go **up** in pitch using the capo – of course the guitar notes go up in pitch, but the vocal part can come down by an octave from the new key.

Transposing without the Capo

Sometimes, to get particular effects, you will need to adjust the pitch of a song without using the capo. When you've chosen the new key, the tonic chord will be the same as the tonic note, but what about the other chords? To find them, some way of counting the interval between the original key and the new one is necessary . . .

First of all, count one for each letter of the musical alphabet. Then, if you **include** both the **original and new tonic notes** (or chords), the interval between say **C** and **G** will be five, or as it's called in music theory, a 'fifth'.

```
C  D  E  F  G   G  A  B  C
1  2  3  4  5   1  2  3  4
```

Thus **C** to **G** is a fifth, and, similarly, **G** to **C** is a fourth.

What would the interval between **A** and **G** be? That's right, counting upward, it would be a seventh. If you take the key up by a certain interval, then the chords you've been using must also go up by the same interval. In the key of C, the common chords are **C, F,** and **G7**. If you change to the key of G, the C chord of course becomes a **G** chord. The **F** and **G7** chords become **C** and **D7** respectively:

```
F  G  A  B  C   G  A  B  C  D
1  2  3  4  5   1  2  3  4  5
```

Note that the **quality** of the chord remains the same, so **G7** becomes not **D** but **D7**.

Another Way

Because music works in patterns, there are always two or more ways of working out the same thing. You can discover the other chords of a new key by finding the intervals between the original tonic chord and its related chords, and counting the same intervals from the new tonic chord. So if you're playing in the key of A, with **A, D,** and **E7** chords, and you change to the key of C . . . **D** and **E7** are a fourth and fifth from **A,** and therefore the new chords will be a fourth and fifth from **C**:

```
 ┌old┐    ┌old┐     ┌new┐     ┌new┐
A B C D   A B C D E7   C D E F   C D E F G7
1 2 3 4   1 2 3 4 5    1 2 3 4   1 2 3 4 5
```

Counting Downward

If the new key is a long way up the musical alphabet from the old one, it may be easier to count the intervals downward. So instead of going up from C to A for example, you'd count down from C to A Then A would be said to be a third below C.

Even More Ideas

Upstrokes after Bass-Strikes

In the bass-strum sections of both Books 1 and 2 there were no upstrokes used immediately after single bass-note strikes by the thumb (or flatpick). For more variety, try and master these patterns in 3/4 and 4/4 that include this technique. technique.
(Do bar after bar until you can do them smoothly.)

3/4 Rhythm. (Any chord.)

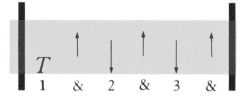

4/4 Rhythm. (Any chord.)

Swing Rhythm

Do you remember the swing rhythm that you used on the two Beatles songs in Book 2? Well, this rhythm can be used in any style that has upstrokes or notes between the beats. The 'straight' rhythm involves playing them exactly halfway between the beats, while for the swing rhythm you delay playing them until **just** before the following beat.
Try playing the two patterns above, first in straight rhythm and then with a swing.

Picking Out the Melody

In Book 2 you played some bass runs, and did other bass-strikes that weren't in the usual place in the bar. Now that you've mastered the common patterns, you need to experiment with hitting the bass on any beat of the bar – in fact, whenever you like. Then you'll soon be able to play the melody of the song (or little 'riffs' – short musical phrases),

while keeping the strums going in between. This can sound very intricate and satisfying, so let's take a look at "Catch The Wind" again, and try Donovan's introduction to his classic song from the sixties . . .

3/4 Rhythm

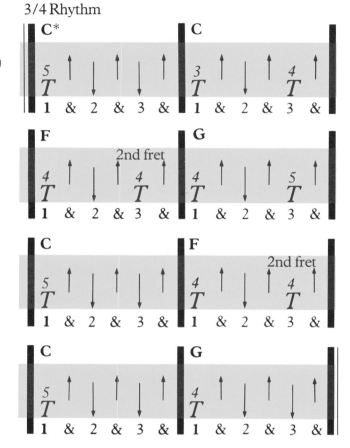

The two **F** bars have two 4th-string notes, one at the beginning of the bar (the first beat), and one at the end (the third beat). The one on the third beat involves moving the left hand from the **F** fingering and placing the second finger on the 2nd fret of the 4th string. The first bass note of the following bar completes a short bass run of sorts. **All** the other bass notes **don't** need a move of the left-hand fingers – the chord is held for the whole bar.

---

*Yes, you'll notice that the key is now C. In the other accompaniment in Book 1, it was in the key of A. The chords you used were **A**, **D**, and **E**. How many steps and semitones have you risen (and also, how many have you fallen if you calculate it that way) to get the chords to **C**, **F**, and **G**? Now try playing the whole song in the new key.

Michael Row The Boat Ashore
Traditional, arranged Russ Shipton

Here's your first gospel song, as well as your first swing rhythm in the bass-strum style. Delay slightly on the downstrokes (strums or single bass notes), and play the upstrums **just** before the following beats, as you did in the swing rhythm for "Yellow Submarine" and "Maxwell's Silver Hammer". Don't play this song too fast.

Try varying the length of the introduction and the 'tags' (the instrumental part between verses) to see

if you prefer different gaps. Also, this is a simple song for you to try to transpose to another key. If your voice would suit a pitch slightly lower, try going down a tone to the key of D. Also remember that you can experiment with using the capo in various places.

Accompaniment 4/4 Swing Rhythm ↓↑ = Strum down/up $\frac{6}{T}$ = Thumb strikes 6th string

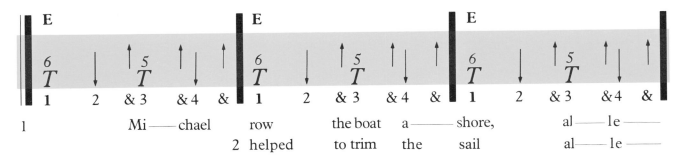

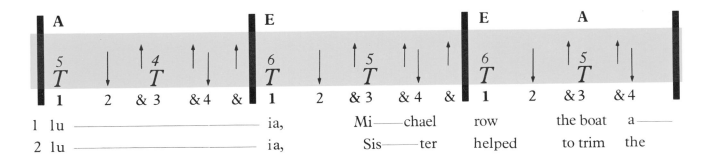

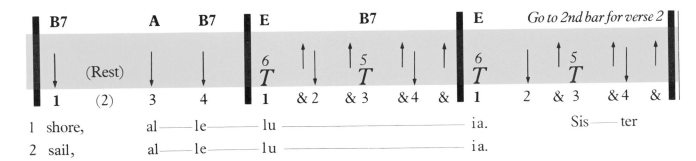

11

Morning Has Broken Cat Stevens

but if you have any problems with it, put your capo on about the 5th fret, and finger the same shapes further up the fretboard. Barre chords are much easier when your arm is nearer your body.

I've put various embellishments and patterns in this accompaniment, so look at and count each bar carefully before playing it. Then go through the whole song very slowly with an even rhythm. Gradually you can speed up, once the chord changes are okay and you can remember the whole accompaniment.

The **G7** chord was included in the chord summary at the back of Book 2, but in case you've forgotten it, here it is again . . .

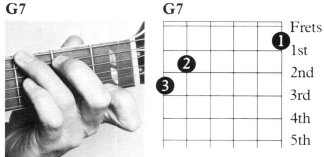

If you finger the **G** chord with the second, third, and fourth fingers (the fourth is shown in the diagram), it's a very easy change from **G** to **G7**. Persevere with this new fingering for the **G** chord, because it will come in very handy for other important left-hand maneuvres.

Here's a beautiful song made popular by Cat Stevens. There's an **F** chord in the accompaniment,

Accompaniment 3/4 Rhythm $\quad \downarrow\uparrow$ = Strum down/up $\quad \overset{4H}{T}$ = Thumb-strike and hammer-on

C	Am	Dm	G
$\overset{5}{T}$ ↓ ↑ ↓	$\overset{5}{T}$ ↑ ↓ ↑ ↓ ↑	$\overset{4}{T}$ ↑ ↓ ↓	$\overset{6}{T}$ ↑ ↓ ↓ ↑
1 2 & 3	1 & 2 & 3 &	1 2 & 3	1 & 2 & 3 &
Morning has bro—	—ken,		like the first

F	C	C	Em
$\overset{6}{T}$ ↓ ↑ ↓	$\overset{5}{T}$ ↑ ↓ ↓ ↑	$\overset{4\frown H}{T}$ ↑ ↓	$\overset{6}{T}$ ↑ ↓ ↑
1 2 & 3	1 & 2 & 3 &	1 & 2 & 3	1 & 2 & 3 &
morn———ing,		blackbird has	spo—

Morning Has Broken   Continued

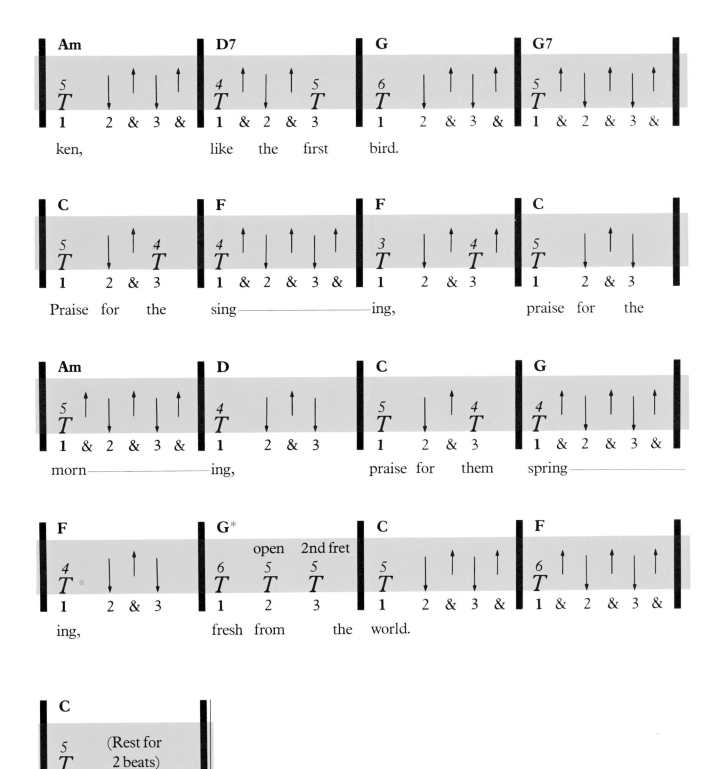

*This is the same bass run from **G** to **C** that you've seen before.

She'll Be Coming Round The Mountain

Traditional,
arranged Russ Shipton

Here's a simple accompaniment for that well-known American traditional song, "She'll Be Coming Round The Mountain." Play and sing this through first, and then I want you to **add bass runs** where I've suggested (and wherever you want to play them). If you get into a mess with either the rhythm or finding the notes of the runs, check back to Book 2 – it's all in there, the bass-strum style section. Also, I want you to add some hammer-ons where you feel they're needed (try the second bars of the same chord). We're back to the key of **A** for this one . . .

Accompaniment 4/4 Rhythm $\uparrow\downarrow$ = Strum down/up $\overset{5}{T}$ = Thumb strikes 5th string

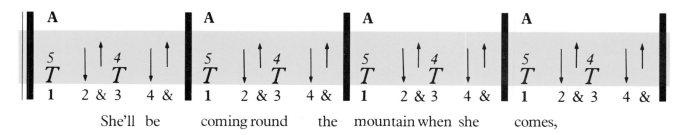

She'll be | coming round | the | mountain when she | comes,

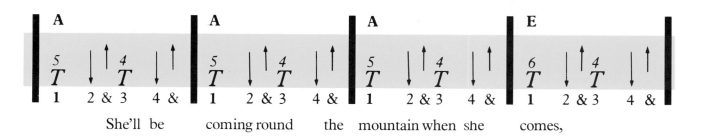

She'll be | coming round | the | mountain when she | comes,

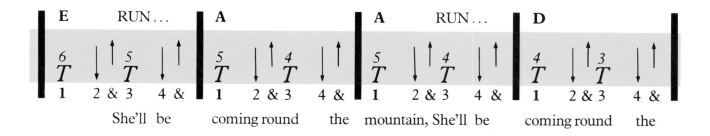

She'll be | coming round | the | mountain, She'll be | coming round | the

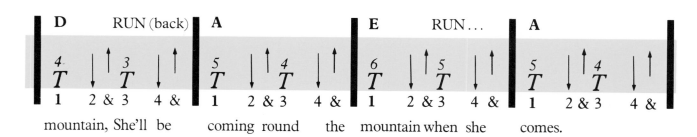

mountain, She'll be | coming round | the | mountain when she | comes.

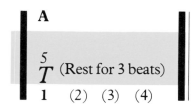

She'll Be Coming Round The Mountain Solo

Now I have something special for you to try – a **complete solo part** to either stand on its own, or be played with the accompaniment on the previous page. Those of you working in the classroom can divide into two groups – those at home can play along with a friend, or even a tape recorder. You may have noticed that the accompaniment is in A and the solo part is in the key of G. That means we have to adjust one to the other with a capo if we're going to play them together–and the easiest way is to get the players with the solo part below to put their capos on at the 2nd fret. Using the **G, C,** and **D7** fingerings, they will actually be playing **A, D,** and **E7** chords.

Solo Part 4/4 Rhythm $\downarrow \uparrow$ = Strum down/up $\overset{3H}{T}$ = Thumb-strike and hammer-on
Capo 2nd Fret, **G** = **A**, **D7** = **E7**, **C** = **D**

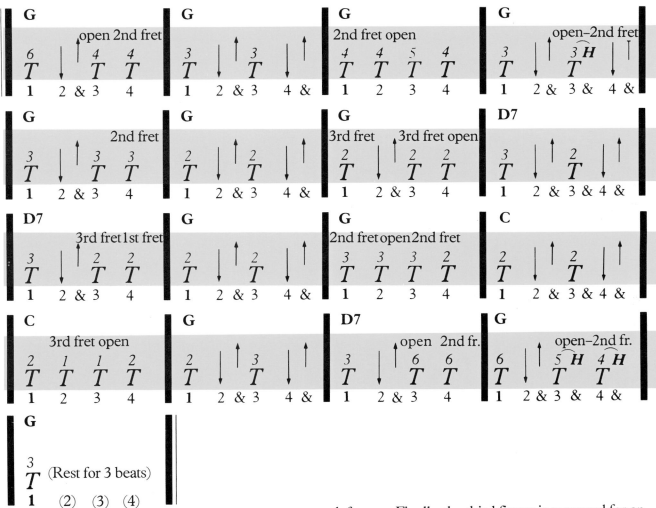

Notes

Finger the chords for each bar as shown, but move the most convenient finger to play these notes that aren't in the chord shape that you're in. These notes are all indicated by fret, above the notation. The strums can be short – use the top **four** strings only. In the **G** bars, use your first finger for the **E** and **A** notes on the 4th and 3rd strings. The other two fingers should remain in position. In bar seven, the third finger is moved to the 2nd string, 3rd fret, for the **D** note, and can be left there for the following down/up strum. The top string is left open. Finally, the third finger is removed for an open 2nd-string **B** note.

In the ninth and thirteenth bars, use your fourth finger for the **D** and **G** notes respectively. The **D7** bar near the end involves a bass run to **G.** As you're playing the open 6th string, bring your first finger up for the **F♯** note on the 6th string 2nd fret. Use your first finger for the two hammer-ons near the end. The first is the normal **G**-chord 5th-string hammer-on, while the other is more unusual – an open 4th-string **D** note to the 2nd-fret **E** note.

Even More Ideas

The Syncopated Arpeggio

This type of pattern has a grand name, but don't let it put you off. It's the same sort of thing as the calypso strum that you tried with "Jamaica Farewell," and once you've got it fixed in your head, you'll soon be able to sing along with it. In fact, have a look at the verse of that song with this sort of accompaniment, and see if you can manage to play it this way as well as with strumming. Then you'll be able to vary what you do during the song. Perhaps you could do this picking style for the verse, and then break into the heavier strumming for the chorus . . .

Jamaica Farewell 4/4 Rhythm

Verse

G			
$\overset{6}{T}$ i m	$\overset{4}{T}$ i m	$\overset{4}{T}$ i	
1 & 2 &	3 & 4 &		

C			
$\overset{5}{T}$ i m	$\overset{4}{T}$ i m	$\overset{4}{T}$ i	
1 & 2 &	3 & 4 &		

D			
$\overset{4}{T}$ i m	$\overset{3}{T}$ i m	$\overset{3}{T}$ i	
1 & 2 &	3 & 4 &		

G			*Repeat 4 bars*
$\overset{6}{T}$ i m	$\overset{4}{T}$ i m	$\overset{4}{T}$ i	
1 & 2 &	3 & 4 &		

As you can tell, this picking pattern is very suitable for the calypso type of song. In a class, some can play the song with a strumming backing, and some with the arpeggio. Then the two groups can swap parts. (At home, a tape recorder can be used as before).

Apart from calypso accompaniments, this syncopated rhythm picking is very well suited to slow ballads – it makes the accompaniment much more interesting without having to add many embellishments. In this section, I'll be giving you the well-known Leonard Cohen song, "Suzanne," with this offbeat style. When you've mastered that try "Sailing" in this style as well.

Pinches

In the alternating thumb section of Book 2, you used the 'pinch' technique. This involves playing two strings at the same time with the right-hand thumb and finger. Let's try a few patterns using pinches in the arpeggio style . . .

4/4 Rhythm

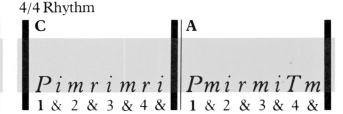

Use the chords indicated first, and then try others. As you did before, pinch with the right-hand thumb and **ring** finger, which plucks the **1st** string. Now have a go at a couple of patterns where the pinch comes not on the first beat, but elsewhere in the bar.

4/4 Rhythm

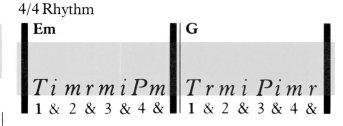

Now think of other patterns apart from all those you've learned so far. Write some down, using pinches and thumb-strikes in different places, to see what they sound like. You could also try doing some pinches with the thumb and **middle** finger, or even thumb and **index** finger. As with all the styles the more different and unusual patterns you master, the nearer you'll be to improvising as you go along. Or at least you'll be able to create some interesting arrangements for songs in the future. So keep experimenting!

Goin' Places   Russ Shipton

So far, you've used the swing rhythm in two styles only–the strumming and bass-strum styles. You can, of course, swing the rhythm in all styles, so here's an instrumental piece with an arpeggio swing pattern. For the swing rhythm, remember to play the notes that lie between the beats **just before** the following beat.

Instrumental 4/4 Swing Rhythm   *Trmi* = thumb, ring, middle, and index fingers

E							open
6					5		
T	r m	i m	r T	i
1	& 2	& 3	& 4	&

A							open
5					4		
T	r m	i m	r T	i
1	& 2	& 3	& 4	&

E						1st fr.
6					5	
T	r m	i m	r T
1	& 2	& 3	& 4

B7						2nd fr. open
5					6	
T	r m	i m	r T	i
1	& 2	& 3	& 4	&

E		E7				open
6				5		
T	r m	i m	T	i
1	& 2	& 3	4	&

A		Am				
5					5	
T	r m	i m	T
1	& 2	& 3	4

E		B7				
6			5			
T	i m	r T	i m	r
1	& 2	& 3	& 4	&

E						
6	4					
T	T i	m r	(Rest)
1	& 2	& 3	4

Notes
When changing chords you can keep the rhythm going by hitting an open string – otherwise you may not get to the next chord in time.

In the third bar, for the last thumb-strike (on the 1st fret, 5th string) use your first finger.

For the last thumb-strike in the fourth bar, use your second finger – move it from the 5th string.

For the 6th bar, try fingering the **A** chord with your second, third, and fourth fingers – that'll make the change to **Am** quite easy.

Sometimes the thumb can play the first two notes in a bar when they are on the bass strings, as in the last bar above.

Where Have All The Flowers Gone? Pete Seeger

I'm sure you all know this famous song. It was given more of a pop treatment a while ago, but the words still carry their forceful message. Many other protest songs followed this classic.

The first part of the verse repeats itself (the chords, not the melody), so I'd like you to learn just the accompaniment given until you can play the whole song smoothly. The pinches have been restricted to the second part on the next page, but when you're happy with the accompaniment as given, try to think of variations for the first part, including different bass runs, pinches, and maybe some hammer-ons.

Accompaniment 4/4 Rhythm   *P* = Pinch thumb and third finger   *T i m r* = Thumb, index, middle, and ring finger

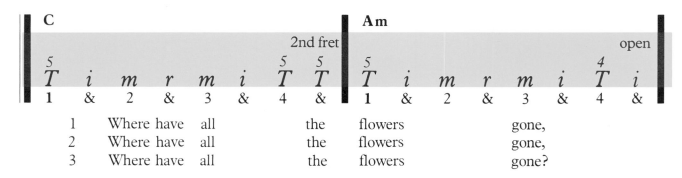

C								Am							
				2nd fret											open
5						5	5	5						4	
T	*i*	*m*	*r*	*m*	*i*	*T*	*T*	*T*	*i*	*m*	*r*	*m*	*i*	*T*	*i*
1	&	2	&	3	&	4	&	1	&	2	&	3	&	4	&

1		Where	have	all			the	flowers				gone,			
2		Where	have	all			the	flowers				gone,			
3		Where	have	all			the	flowers				gone?			

Notes

I hope you remember how the system of fingers and strings works – the right-hand index finger plays the 3rd string, the middle plays the 2nd string, and the ring plays the 1st string. (Later you can vary this strict rule, but it's necessary for the moment.)

As I said above, when you've mastered this accompaniment, try using your own ideas for bass runs, hammer-ons, and pinches, plus mixing up different patterns.

Try a **Dm** chord instead of the **F**, on the first repeat of the four bars -- it's a nice variation.

Where Have All The Flowers Gone? Continued

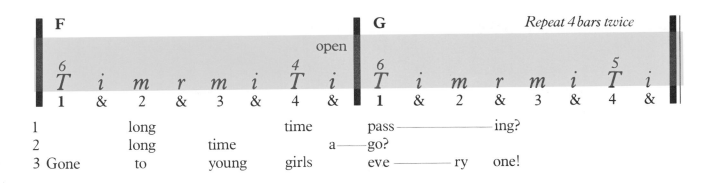

1		long				time		pass ——————— ing?							
2		long		time				a —— go?							
3 Gone		to		young		girls		eve ——— ry		one!					

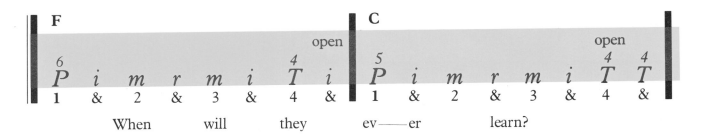

When will they ev —— er learn?

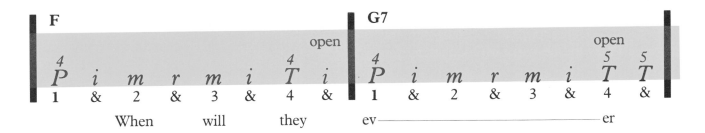

When will they ev ——————————————— er

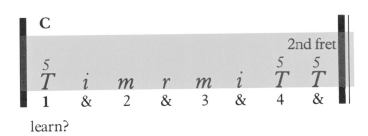

learn?

Now repeat the **Am**, **F**, and **G** bars, but just
instrumentally. Then go into the second verse.

Notes
Remember that the pinches involve the thumb and
ring finger, which plays the 1st string.
Where a note isn't in the chord you're fingering, I've
shown the fret above the notation.
At the end of the **Am** and **F** bars I've indicated an
open 3rd string played by the index finger. This will
help you to get to the next chord more easily, and
doesn't sound bad.

Suzanne   Leonard Cohen

Many of Leonard Cohen's tunes are not renowned for their lilting melodies, but this is the most frequently recorded exception. All his songs are very haunting and intense, and to help this atmosphere the accompaniment below is largely played on the middle strings. As mentioned in the section's introduction page, this accompaniment involves a bass, thumb-strike **off** the beat, as shown

in the alternative verse arrangement for "Jamaica Farewell." Give each note equal time and you'll get the right effect.

As for "Where Have All The Flowers Gone," some variations and embellishments are used, but after you've learned this accompaniment, try to put some ideas of your own into it.

Two chords that you haven't come across are used here, one's a barre chord, but the other's a bit easier. (Perhaps you tried the **Bm** in "Moon Shadow"?) . . .

The **B** Minor Chord   The **D** Ninth Chord

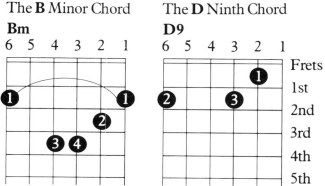

Accompaniment 4/4 Rhythm   *P* = Pinch thumb and ring finger   *T i m* = Thumb, index, and middle finger

Verse

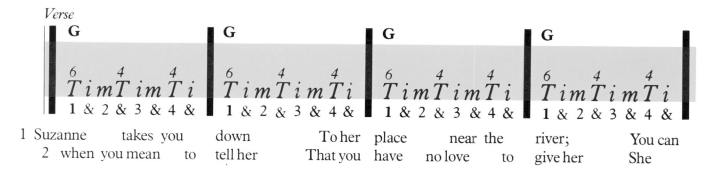

1 Suzanne   takes you   down   To her   place   near the   river;   You can
2 when you mean   to   tell her   That you have   no love   to   give her   She

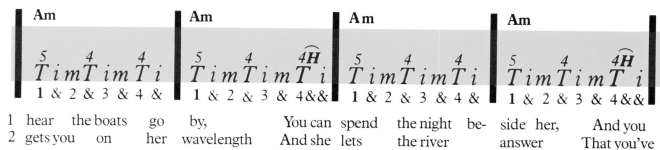

1 hear   the boats   go   by,   You can spend   the night   be-   side her,   And you
2 gets you   on   her   wavelength   And she lets   the river   answer   That you've

Notes
The hammer-ons are quick ones, as you've had before in the arpeggio style.

20

Suzanne Continued

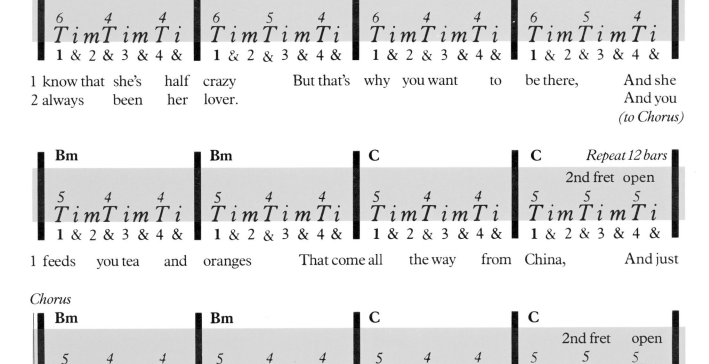

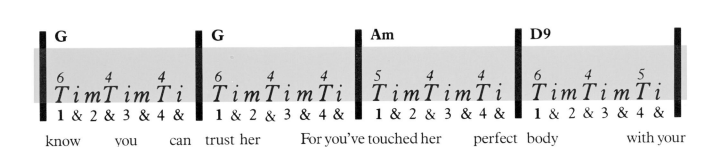

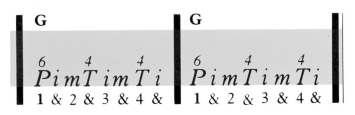

Notes

You go to the chorus after the repeat of the **whole** third line of the verse.

Go carefully over the pinch bars – the pattern's slightly different.

There are three bass notes in the **D9** bar. This **D9** chord is quite similar to the **D7** chord, except it has an open 1st string i.e. an **E** note added.

Watch out for the change of bass in the top line on this page.

Some New Ideas

More Patterns

In Book 2 we used two simple patterns for "Freight Train" and "If I Were A Carpenter," and then I gave you a couple more patterns at the end of the section. Before you get to it, have a look at this pattern, the main one that's used in the "Streets Of London" accompaniment . . .

C

5	4	5	4
P	i T	m T	i T
1 &	2 &	3 &	4

And now try this one:

G7

6	4	6	4	
T	T	T i	T	m
1	2	3 &	4	&

Remember you're playing **just** the top two treble strings as shown for this style in Book Two.

Treble Hammer-Ons

Finally we've come to the time when you're ready to tackle some hammer-ons on the treble strings. They're a bit harder than those on the bass, but now you've had a lot of practice, the treble strings shouldn't be so hard to press down. In the alternating thumb style, most of the hammer-ons come with a bass note as well, and usually at the start of a bar, like this . . .

D

4	3	4	3
P ⌢ H	T i	T m	T
1 &	2 &	3 &	4

A

5	4	5	4
P ⌢ H	T m	T i	T
1 &	2 &	3 &	4

Because this is simple notation, you'll have to remember that the hammer-on sign is for a treble string when **below** the bass-string number. With the **D** chord, the string to be hammered is normally the 1st, unless otherwise stated. With the **A,** the string will be the 2nd.

First of all, try a hammer-on on the 1st string, from open to 2nd fret, using your left-hand first finger. Then try it with your second finger. Don't forget to come down quickly and firmly, otherwise you'll damp the string and lose the sound. Then finger the whole **D** chord, and try again. Finally, play the whole bar above, counting it steadily – the hammer-on must come exactly halfway between beats. Now do the same thing with the **A** chord, hammering on the open to 2nd fret, 2nd string.

Mixing Patterns

Take one bar of one pattern, and alternate it with a different one, and you'll be well on the way to an interesting accompaniment with some dynamics. So try these examples . . .

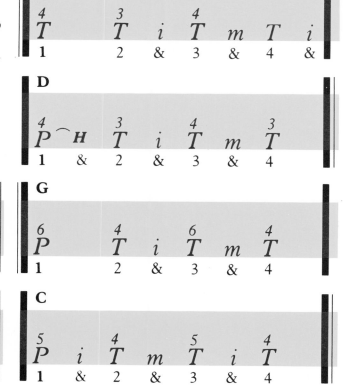

D

4	3	4	
T	T i	T m	T i
1	2 &	3 &	4 &

D

4	3	4	3
P ⌢ H	T i	T m	T
1 &	2 &	3 &	4

G

6	4	6	4
P	T i	T m	T
1	2 &	3 &	4

C

5	4	5	4
P	i T	m T	i T
1 &	2 &	3 &	4

This Train   Traditional, arranged Russ Shipton

Here's a spiritual for you to get back into this alternating thumb style. I've left the accompaniment quite simple, with just two patterns one after the other – you'll see how that gives some pace to the rhythm.
For the **D** to **D7** bars, you could try fingering the **D** chord like this . . .

It's much easier to go from **D** to **D7** if you use this fingering. In time, you must experiment with slightly different fingerings for most chords to suit the particular arrangements and changes.

Take this accompaniment quite fast when you've got the basic idea. Put a bit of bounce into the right-hand thumb-strikes too! (**Not** swing but spring.)

Before going on to the next song, I'd like you to transpose the song below to another key. For many of you it is probably too high (or low) anyway.

Now go back to "Blowin' In The Wind," and rearrange the accompaniment in the alternating thumb style. Use two patterns in the same way as I've done for "This Train."

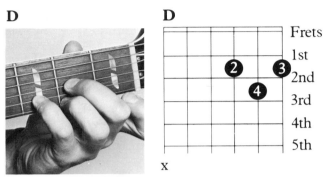

D

D

Frets
1st
2nd
3rd
4th
5th

x

Accompaniment 4/4 Rhythm   *T i m* = Thumb, index, and middle fingers

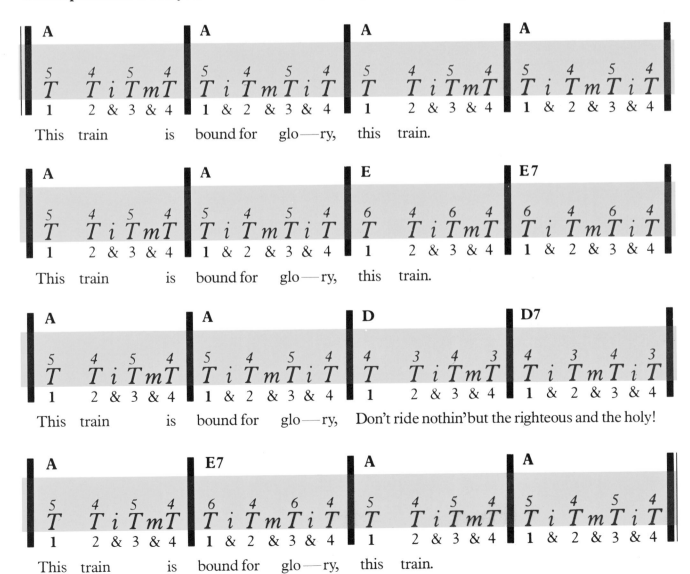

Streets Of London   Ralph McTell

This song was written in 1967, but enjoyed worldwide acclaim about ten years later. The words have a simple but important message to relate, and the tune flows along beautifully. Ralph McTell uses the alternating thumb style a lot, but this accompaniment seems to fit the song particularly well. In my other books (*Folk Guitar Styles of Today* series) you'll find an arrangement quite similar to the one Ralph himself uses, and other more advanced accompaniments for many well-known songs, but here we'll stick to certain patterns.

First of all, take the pattern in the first bar, and use that for the whole song. Then, when you're happy with that, try to vary the accompaniment in the ways I have shown – go through bar by bar carefully so you don't miss anything. After you've mastered this arrangement, try adding some ideas of your own.

Accompaniment 4/4 Rhythm   *P* = Pinch thumb and middle finger   *T i m* = Thumb, index, and middle finger

Verse

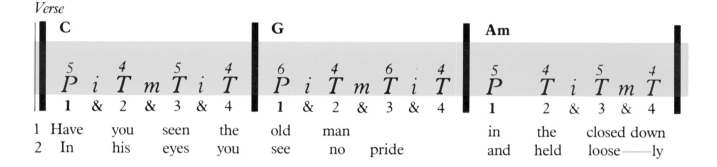

1 Have   you   seen   the   old   man   in   the   closed down
2 In   his   eyes   you   see   no   pride   and   held   loose——ly

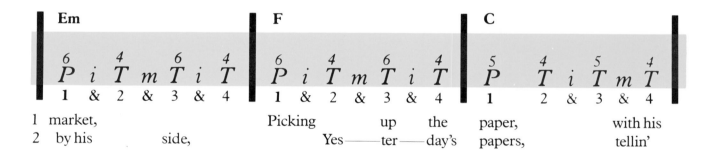

1 market,   Picking   up   the   paper,   with his
2 by his   side,   Yes——ter——day's   papers,   tellin'

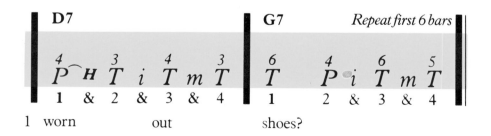

1 worn   out   shoes?

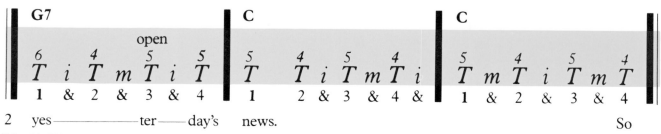

2 yes————ter——day's   news.   So

Streets Of London Continued

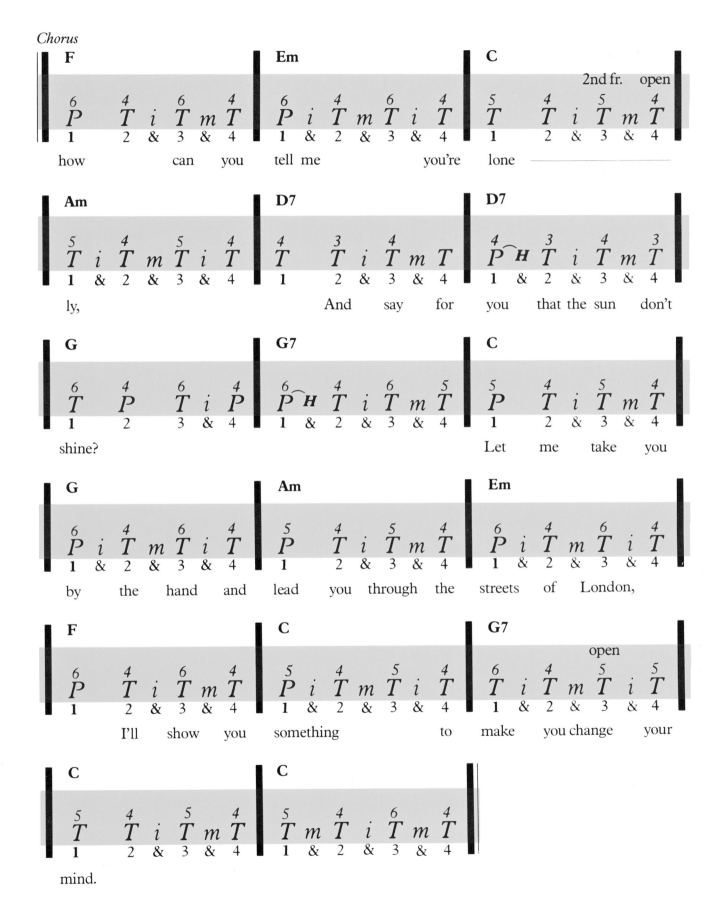

Chorus

F
how — can you — tell me — you're — lone

Em

C 2nd fr. open

Am
ly,

D7
And — say — for — you

D7
that the sun — don't

G
shine?

G7

C
Let — me — take — you

G
by — the — hand — and

Am
lead — you — through — the

Em
streets — of — London,

F
I'll — show — you

C
something — to

G7 open
make — you change — your

C
mind.

C

Take Me Home Country Roads
Bill Danoff, Taffy Nivert and John Denver

Here's a song that's folk, country, and pop all at the same time. It has a great melody, but quite a range is involved – maybe you'll need to put your capo on the 4th or 5th fret, like I do.

I haven't bothered with introductions up to now, because you've had enough other things to think about, but some sort of instrumental lead-in is likely to improve the presentation of any song. Perhaps a sequence direct from the chorus or verse, or a similar, short chord sequence like the one

below, would be enough. Normally the introduction shouldn't be too long. Experiment with lead-ins for some of the songs you've learned so far.

Another thing I haven't mentioned much is tempo. Different people like to play the same songs at different speeds. Experiment with various patterns, styles, and speeds – then stick with the combination that suits you and the song best!

Accompaniment 4/4 Rhythm $\overset{\frown}{PH}$ = Pinch and treble hammer-on $\overset{\overset{5}{\frown}H}{T}$ = Thumb and bass hammer-on
Tim = Thumb, index, and middle fingers

Introduction

D	**D**	**A**	**A**
4 3 4 3	4 3 4 3	5 4 5 4	5 4 5 4
P T i T m T	P̂H T i T m T	P T i T m T	P̂H T m T i T
1 2 & 3 & 4	1 & 2 & 3 & 4	1 2 & 3 & 4	1 & 2 & 3 & 4

(roads.)

G	**G**	open–2nd fret **D**	
6 4 6 4	6 4 5 H 4 H	4 3 4 3	
P T i T m T i	T P T T	T T i T m T i	
1 2 & 3 & 4 &	1 2 3 & 4 &	1 2 & 3 & 4 &	

Apart from an intro, you can use this as a tag at the end of the chorus.

Notes
Remember that the hammer-on sign above the bass-string number means a bass hammer-on. When it's **below** it means a treble hammer-on. The third beat in the second **G** bar of the intro

involves a usual bass hammer-on. The fourth beat is a hammer-on from the open 4th string to the 2nd fret. For this, use your first finger. In this case, you can take your other fingers off, ready for moving to the **D** chord.

26

Take Me Home Country Roads Continued

Verse

D	D	Bm	Bm
4⌢ 3 4 3	4 3 4 3	5 4 5 4	5 4 5 4
P**H** T i T m T	T T i T m T	P T i T m T	P T i T m T
1 & 2 & 3 & 4	1 2 & 3 & 4	1 & 2 & 3 & 4	1 2 & 3 & 4

1   Al—most   hea———ven,   West Vir———gin———ia,
2   Life   is   old   there,   old—er than the   trees,

A	A	G	D *Repeat first 7 bars*
5 4 5 4	5⌢ 4 5 4	6 4 4 5	4 3 4 3
P T i T m T	P**H** T i T m T	P T i T m T	P T i T m T i
1 2 & 3 & 4	1 & 2 & 3 & 4	1 2 & 3 & 4	1 & 2 & 3 4 &

1   the Blue Ridge   Moun———tains, the   Shen-an—do—ah   Riv———er.
2   younger than the   moun———tains,   blow-ing like   a   *(to Chorus)*

Chorus

D	D	D	A
4	4 3 4 3	4⌢ 3 4 3	5 4 5 4
P (Rest for 3 beats)	P T i T m T	P**H** T i T m T	P T i T m T
1 (2) (3) (4)	1 2 & 3 & 4	1 & 2 & 3 & 4	1 2 & 3 & 4

breeze. Coun—try   roads,   take   me   home

A	Bm	Bm	G
5⌢ 4 5 4	5 4 5 4	5⌢ ★4 5 4	6 4 6
P**H** T m T i T	P T i T m T	P**H** T m T i T	P T i T m T
1 & 2 & 3 & 4	1 2 & 3 & 4	1 & 2 & 3 & 4	1 2 & 3 & 4

to   the   place   where   I   be———long,

G	D	D	A
6 4 6 5	4 3 4 3	4⌢ 3 4 3	5 4 5 4
T i T m T i T	T T i T m T i	P**H** T i T m T	P T i T m T i
1 & 2 & 3 & 4	1 2 & 3 & 4 &	1 & 2 & 3 & 4	1 2 & 3 & 4 &

West Vir———ginia,   mountain   momma,

A	G	G	
5⌢ 4 5 4	6 4 6 4	6 4 6 5	
P**H** T m T i T	P T i T m T i	T i T m T i T	
1 & 2 & 3 & 4	1 2 & 3 & 4 &	1 & 2 & 3 & 4	

take   me   home,   count———ry

Return to the first bar on
the previous page for
"roads,"

★This treble hammer-on is from the 2nd to 3rd fret on the 2nd string.

Some More Ideas

Classical compositions aren't so pattern like as the modern styles you've been learning. Partly because they usually stand on their own as instrumentals (and must therefore have variations from bar to bar, and section to section), and partly because they don't involve the normal heavy beat stress of popular music today.

So far, you've tried just one classical piece, and that was a simple, one-note-at-a-time arrangement. On these next few pages there are some intermediate level compositions, which explore some more ideas of the classical guitar style. If you follow my notes carefully you shouldn't find them too difficult. Take them very slowly and deliberately at first.

To begin with, let's have a look at a study by Fernando Carulli, written about 150 years ago. It's in 3/4 rhythm: the *3* means that there are three beats in each bar, and the *4* means that each of the three beats has the time value of a quarter note. As in the songs, stress the first beat, a little more than the others.

Study   Fernando Carulli

Instrumental 3/4 Rhythm   Standard music notation – see pages 4 and 27 of Book 2
T i m = Thumb, index, and middle fingers of the right hand

This sign means rest for one quarter note (i.e. one beat)

Notes
Key and Chords – Because there are no sharp (or flat) signs at the start of each line of notation, the piece must be in the key of C. Thus the first and last chord will almost certainly be **C** major. See if you can work out which chord is involved for each bar. (Page 5 has details of chord notes if you've forgotten.)
Fingers – Classical players use only the left-hand fingers they need at any one time. So in these pieces you can forget about fingering the whole of the chord shapes. Work out which fingers are strictly necessary, and use only those – economical use of fingers makes for smoother playing.
Decisions – Sometimes there is a choice of finger to use. Experiment with different possibilities, and choose the one that suits you best. For example, you can use the first and third fingers in the 4th bar above, or the second and fourth instead. And in the seventh bar, the second finger can be used for the low **G** note, with the first playing the **A** note that follows, or you could use the third and second.
Applications – Many ideas in classical compositions can be used for arrangements of accompaniments to modern songs. In this case, the bass-pluck pattern in some of the bars can be used very successfully in humorous, or story-type folk songs. Try it for "Happy Birthday" and "There's A Hole In The Bucket."

28

Passing Note Waltz Russ Shipton

The study on the previous page was written as **one part,** but really the music involves **two distinct parts** – the treble (melody) and the bass (rhythm and harmony). In the piece below, I've separated the bass and treble parts by using note stems that go down and up respectively. You'll see that each part must add up to three quarter-notes worth of time (three beats here) for each bar. Work out the timing of each part and then put them together.

This is another instrumental in 3/4 rhythm, and uses just one sign that you don't know – the dot after a note means that the note is half as long again in time value. So the half-notes that have a dot after them must last for 1½ half-notes, or three quarter-notes' time-value (i.e. three beats, which here is one bar). There is a pause in the treble part during the sixth bar, so the quarter rest sign is used for the second beat.

Instrumental 3/4 Rhythm, Standard music notation – see pages 4 and 27 of Book 2.
T i m r = Thumb, index, middle, and ring fingers of right hand

Notes
What major scale has two sharps (**F♯** and **C♯**) in it? Well, that's the key for this one. Now try to find the chords, as before.
The treble 'passing' notes (or run notes) are quite easy to find – raise a finger that's down, or add another (i.e. in the third and sixth bars you can add your third finger for the **D** note on the 2nd string). When you've played it using the full chord shapes that you know, have another look at the notes you're actually playing, and see which left-hand fingers you **really** need.

29

Another study in the classical style follows on the next page. As the title suggests, it involves a switch from a treble to a bass line and back again – a sort of question and answer arrangement that's used in most forms of music from time to time. I've heard it in Indian music, pop and blues, and also in opera. This piece is not very long or tricky, but should give you useful practice in right-hand flexibility and accuracy. Some points about the notation need to be explained first. Then I'll give you some suggestions regarding both left- and right-hand fingering.

Rests

As well as signs for the various lengths of notes, there need to be signs for different amounts of silence. The notes are shown on page 4 of Book 2, and so far you've seen one rest sign – the quarter rest. Here are the important ones all together . . .

> ⁊ = eighth rest
>
> ⸸ = quarter rest
>
> ▬ = half rest
> (when placed on **top** of a staff line)
>
> ▬ = whole rest
> (when placed under a staff line)

Dotted Notes

In the "Passing Note Waltz," you came across the dotted half-note. A half-note with a dot following means that it lasts for 1½ half-notes', or three quarter-notes', time. The same thing happens to other notes (or rests) when a dot follows them – they last half as long again. So the dotted quarter-note lasts for three eighth-notes' time-value.

2/4 Rhythm

So far in this course you've seen just two rhythms – the 4/4 and 3/4 rhythms. Concentrating on just two time signatures probably made it easier to master the material presented so far, but sooner or later other rhythms will crop up, especially in classical music, and you'll need to know how to read the notation for them.

The top number in a time signature, as it's known, signifies the number of beats in each measure, or bar. Tapping your foot on these beats certainly helps to get the rhythm right, and stressing the **first** beat in each bar usually creates the effect that's needed. The bottom number of a time signature tells you how **long** each beat must last. Thus in the case of 2/4, there are two beats in each bar (and you stress the first of each two), and each beat must last for one quarter-note. If the bottom number were an *8*, each beat would last just one eighth-note. Had it been a *2*, each beat would last one half-note. But these rhythms will be examined in Book 4. Pictorially, the 2/4 rhythm will generally be stressed like this . . . **1**& 2& **1**& 2& **1**& 2& **1**& 2& etc.

Fingering ("Call and Answer")

The first bar involves a **G** chord, and the second a **D** chord – here you can start off using the full **G** chord followed by the **D9** chord fingering that I showed you a while back. Then try to use just the fingers needed. Bars six and seven aren't easy, but again use the full chord shapes to begin with: **C** then **E7** then **A.**

The same thing applies to right-hand fingering as it did for the left – experiment with different possibilities, and use the fingering that suits you and the piece. Particularly with notes on the same string, though, you should use alternate fingers, otherwise the result could be a jerky rhythm.

Sixth Bar

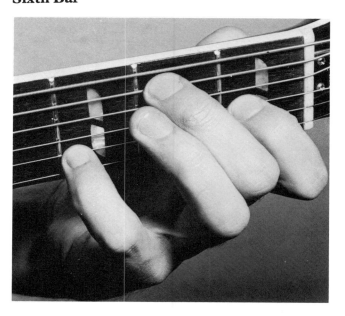

Call And Answer Russ Shipton

Instrumental 2/4 Rhythm   Standard music notation – see pages 4 and 27, Book 2.
T i m r = Thumb, index, middle, and ring fingers of right hand

Notes
In the first bar, let the bass ring for the whole
duration (i.e. for two beats), while in the second bar
make sure the treble note rings for the full bar.
The sharp sign at the start of each line of notation
means you're in the key of G. There are two
'accidentals' (called so because they're not in the
major scale of G) in the sixth and seventh bars, so
they have a sharp sign just before them.

Lyrics

Moon Shadow

Chorus:
I'm being followed by a moon shadow, moon
shadow, moon shadow.
Leapin' and hoppin' on a moon shadow, moon
shadow, moon shadow.
Verse 1:
And if I ever lose my hands,
Lose my power lose my hands,
Oh if I ever lose my hands,
Oh, oh, oh, oh,
I won't have to work no more.
Middle Section:
(And) did it take long to find me?
I asked the faithful light.
Did it take long to find me?
And are you gonna stay the night? (Oh)
Verse 2:
And if I ever lose my eyes,
If my color all runs dry,
Yes if I ever lose my eyes,
Oh, oh, oh, oh,
I won't have to cry no more.
Verse 3:
And if I ever lose my legs,
I won't moan and I won't beg,
Oh if I ever lose my legs,
Oh, oh, oh, oh,
I won't have to walk no more.
Verse 4:
And if I ever lose my mouth,
All my teeth, north and south,
Yes if I ever lose my mouth,
Oh, oh, oh, oh,
I won't have to talk

Jamaica Farewell

Verse 1:
Down the way where the nights are gay
And the sun shines daily on the mountain top,
I took a trip on a sailing ship
And when I reached Jamaica I made a stop.
Chorus:
But I'm sad to say that I'm on my way,
Won't be back for many a day.
My heart is down, my head is turning around,
I had to leave a little girl in Kingston town.
Verse 2:
Down in the market you can hear
Ladies cry out as on their heads they bear
Akkai rice, salt fish are nice
And the rum is fine any time of year.

Verse 3:
Sounds of laughter everywhere
And the dancing girls swing to and fro.
I must declare my heart is there
Though I've been from Maine to Mexico.

Michael Row The Boat Ashore

Verse 1:
Michael row the boat ashore, alleluia,
Michael row the boat ashore, alleluia.
Verse 2:
Sister helped to trim the sail, alleluia,
Sister helped to trim the sail, alleluia.
Verse 3:
The river Jordan is chilly and cold, alleluia,
Chills the body, but not the soul, alleluia.
Verse 4:
The river Jordan is deep and wide, alleluia,
Milk and honey on the other side, alleluia.

Morning Has Broken

Verse 1:
Morning has broken, like the first morning,
Blackbird has spoken like the first bird,
Praise for the singing, praise for the morning,
Praise for them springing, fresh from the world.
Verse 2:
Sweet the rain's new fall, sunlit from heaven,
Like the first dew fall on the first grass,
Praise for the sweetness of the wet garden,
Sprung in completeness, where his feet pass.
Verse 3:
Mine is the sunlight, mine is the morning,
Born of the one light Eden saw play,
Praise with elation, praise every morning,
God's recreation of the new day.

She'll Be Coming Round The Mountain

Verse 1:
She'll be coming round the mountain when she
comes, *(2x)*
She'll be coming round the mountain *(2x)*
She'll be coming round the mountain when she
comes.
Verse 2:
She'll be driving six white horses when she
comes *(2x)*
She'll be driving six white horses *(2x)*
She'll be driving six white horses when she comes.

Verse 3:
She'll be wearing pink pajamas when she
comes *(2 x)*
She'll be wearing pink pajamas *(2 x)*
She'll be wearing pink pajamas when she comes.
Verse 4:
She will have to sleep with Grandma when she
comes *(2x)*
She will have to sleep with Grandma *(2x)*
She will have to sleep with Grandma when she
comes.
Verse 5:
And we'll all go to meet her when she comes *(2 x)*
And we'll all go to meet her *(2x)*
Oh we'll all go to meet her when she comes.

Where Have All The Flowers Gone?

Verse 1:
Where have all the flowers gone, long time
passing?
Where have all the flowers gone, long time ago?
Where have all the flowers gone?
Gone to young girls every one!
When will they ever learn? When will they ever
learn?
Verse 2:
Where have all the young girls gone, long time
passing?
Where have all the young girls gone, long time ago?
Where have all the young girls gone?
Gone to young men every one!
When will they ever learn? When will they ever
learn?
Verse 3:
Where have all the young men gone, long time
passing?
Where have all the young men gone, long time ago?
Where have all the young men gone?
Gone to soldiers, every one!
When will they ever learn? When will they ever
learn?
Verse 4:
And where have all the soldiers gone, long time
passing?
Where have all the soldiers gone, a long time ago?
Where have all the soldiers gone?
Gone to graveyards, every one!
When will they ever learn? When will they ever
learn?
Verse 5:
And where have all the graveyards gone, long time
passing?
Where have all the graveyards gone, long time ago?

Where have all the graveyards gone?
Gone to flowers, every one!
When will they ever learn? When will they ever
learn?

Suzanne

Verse 1:
Suzanne takes you down
To her place near the river;
You can hear the boats go by,
You can spend the night beside her,
And you know that she's half crazy
But that's why you want to be there,
And she feeds you tea and oranges
That come all the way from China,
And just when you mean to tell her
That you have no love to give her
She gets you on her wavelength
And she lets the river answer
That you've always been her lover.
Chorus:
And you want to travel with her,
And you want to travel blind,
And you know you can trust her
For you've touched her perfect body
with your mind.
Verse 2:
And Jesus was a sailor
When he walked upon the water,
And he spent a long time watching
From his lonely wooden tower,
And when he knew for certain
Only drowning men could see him
He said, "All men will be sailors then
Until the sea shall free them."
But he himself was broken
Long before the sky would open;
Foresaken, almost human,
He sank beneath your wisdom like a stone.
Verse 3:
Now Suzanne takes your hand
And she leads you to the river;
She is wearing rags and feathers
From Salvation Army counters.
And the sun pours down like honey
On our lady of the harbour;
And she shows you where to look
Among the garbage and the flowers.
There are heroes in the seaweed,
There are children in the morning,
They are leaning out for love
And they will lean that way forever,
While Suzanne holds the mirror.

33

Lyrics

This Train

Verse 1:
This train is bound for glory, this train.
This train is bound for glory, this train.
This train is bound for glory,
Don't ride nothin' but the righteous and the holy!
This train is bound for glory, this train.

Verse 2:
This train don't carry no gamblers, this train. *(2x)*
This train don't carry no gamblers,
No midnight ramblers, no bar fliers!
This train is bound for glory, this train.

Verse 3:
This train don't carry no liars, this train. *(2 x)*
This train don't carry no liars,
No hypocrites, and no bar fliers!
This train is bound for glory, this train.

Verse 4:
This train don't carry white or black, this train. *(2 x)*
This train don't carry white or black,
Everybody's treated all alike!
This train is bound for glory, this train.

Streets Of London

Verse 1:
Have you seen the old man in the closed down market,
Picking up the paper, with his worn out shoes?
In his eyes you see no pride and held loosely by his side,
Yesterday's papers tellin' yesterday's news.

Chorus:
So how can you tell me you're lonely,
And say for you that the sun don't shine?
Let me take you by the hand and lead you through the streets of London,
I'll show you something to make you change your mind.

Verse 2:
Have you seen the old gal who walks the streets of London,
Dirt in her hair and her clothes in rags?
She's no time for talking, she just keeps right on walking
Carrying her home in two carrier bags.

Verse 3:
And in the all-night café, at a quarter past eleven
Some old man sitting there on his own?
Looking at the world over the rim of his teacup
Each tea lasts an hour, then he wanders home alone.

Verse 4:
And have you seen the old man outside the Seaman's mission,
His memory's fading with those medal ribbons that he wears?
And in our winter city the rain cries a little pity
For one more forgotten hero and a world that doesn't care.

Take Me Home Country Roads

Verse 1:
Almost heaven, West Virginia, the Blue Ridge Mountains, the Shenandoah river.
Life is old there, older than the trees, younger than the mountains, blowing like a breeze.

Chorus:
Country roads, take me home to the place where I belong,
West Virginia, mountain momma, take me home, country roads.

Middle Section:
I hear her voice, in the morning how she calls me,
The radio reminds me of my home far away.
Drivin' down the road I get a feelin' that I should be home
Yesterday, yesterday.

Verse 2:
All my memories gather round her, a river's lady and a stranger to blue water,
Dark and dusty, painted on the sky, the misty taste of moonshine on the teardrop in my eye.

The Complete Guitar Player

by Russ Shipton.

Songs and music in this book
Air in C: Fernando Sor
And I Love Her
Dance
Down By The Brook
Freight Train
Greensleeves
If You Could Read My Mind
Little Ben
Mellow Yellow
Romanza
Skateboarding In The Park
Streets Of London
Study: Carcassi
Study: Fernando Sor
Sunday Blues
Watermelon

Amsco Publications   New York/London/Sydney/Cologne

Chord Sequences

The Four-Bar Norm

Most musical phrases are contained within a time period of four or eight bars. Though there are exceptions, almost all verses and choruses will involve a multiple of four bars. Check the songs you know, and see if you can discover just how many songs follow similar chord patterns and lengths.

Below I've shown a typical chord sequence of a modern, folk, or even classical piece of music, in a four-bar form ...

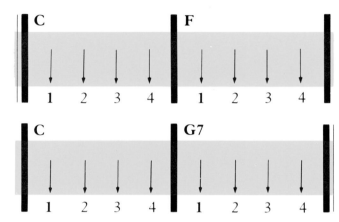

First of all, I'd like you to play this same, short sequence with a more interesting strum pattern than I've shown. Then convert it into bass-strum, arpeggio, and finally alternating thumb style. Now I want you to write out the sequence in the other keys you know, ie. in D,E,G, and A. If you're still a bit shaky on transposing, check back to page 9 of Book 3 (and maybe pages 4 and 5 as well, together with page 4 of Book 2). This is a very important exercise, because when you find sheet music, or are given songs in the future, you'll often want to change the key to one that suits your vocal range, or one that brings out the best guitar sounds for the particular song.

Twelve-Bar Blues

It's hard to say exactly how much influence the traditional blues music of the guitar and piano players in North America had on the popular forms that followed, but it's enough to say that a lot of music today owes a lot to the blues. Apart from the blues being a very important factor in the development of modern music, it's an extremely useful form for learning chord sequences, transposition, different styles of picking and

strumming, including lead guitar techniques, but that's beyond the scope of this course.

The most common form of the blues is the twelve-bar sequence, and the most common twelve-bar sequence is shown below, in the key of E, a popular key for the blues. We'll use this progression as a framework for transposing, so you get to learn something about the blues and chord sequences at the same time ...

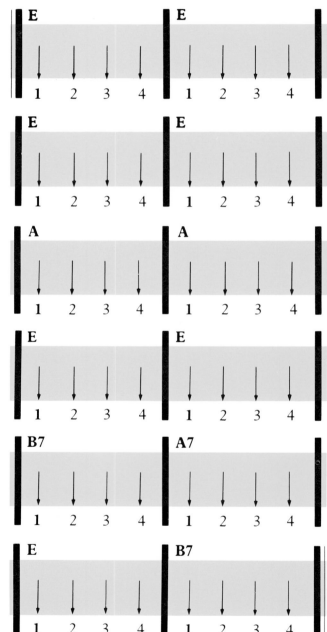

Play through the sequence with a strumming pattern. Now try swinging the rhythm. A swing is often used in blues though not so much in rock music. Then go on to doing picking patterns. In a classroom, some can try strumming, and others a picking style. Once you're used to the feel of the blues, transpose the above sequence to other keys you know as you did with the four-bar sequence.

Ragtime

Another very important branch of traditional music that's related to blues is ragtime – begun by pianists and taken on by guitarists. The two sequences below give you some idea of the chord sequences involved. Try them in the strumming and various picking styles . . .

4/4 Swing

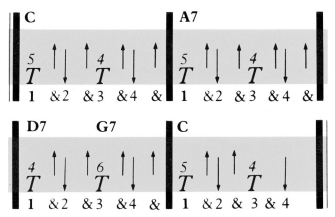

Use the swing rhythm to begin with, then try the sequence with a straight rhythm. Then transpose to the other keys – the sequence below is a transposition of the one in **C** above, with a small change at the start. Don't try to 'de-swing' the rhythm for the picking pattern in the first bar, because with all those pinches, the rhythm must be swung . . .

4/4 Swing

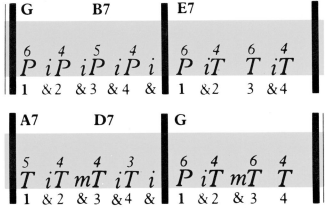

More Chords

Dominant Seventh Chords

All the seventh chords you've learned so far (**A7**, **B7**, **D7**, **E7**, and **G7**), are known as 'dominant seventh' chords. If you use that name for them, you'll be able to distinguish them from the other seventh chords I show below. Let's first have a look at two dominant seventh chords that you haven't seen yet . . .

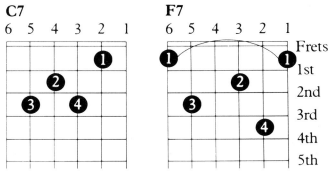

The **C7** Chord is not very difficult–just add your 4th finger on the 3rd string after holding the usual **C** chord.

Minor Seventh Chords

The minor seventh chords serve the same type of function as the dominant seventh chords – and the **same note is added** to the normal minor chord as the one added to the major chord for the dominant seventh. So to change an **Am** chord to an **Am7** chord, we add the **G** note, as we did to get the **A7** chord from the normal **A** major chord . . .

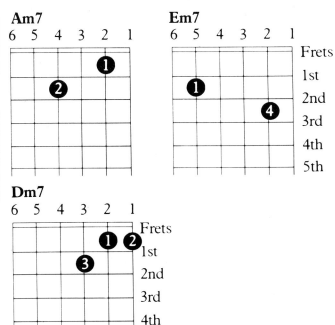

More Chords Continued

Major Seventh Chords

One of the most important chords in jazz music is the major seventh chord. Along with other much more complicated chords, it has a very "unfinished" feel about it – it !eaves things "up in the air." This chord is extremely useful even in folk and pop music as a substitute for the usual major chord. First let's see six of the major seventh chords, most of which are quite straightforward to finger ...

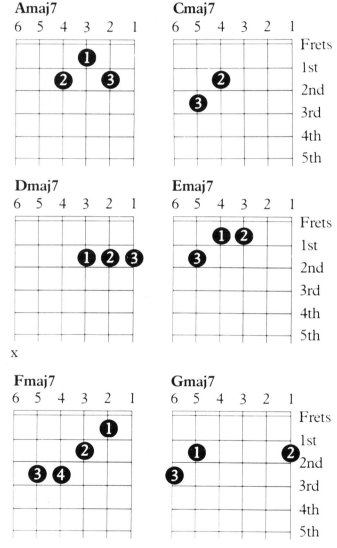

Amaj7   Cmaj7

Dmaj7   Emaj7

x

Fmaj7   Gmaj7

See what I mean by "up in the air"? Well, have another look at one of the songs in the first book: "Leaving On A Jet Plane." Sticking to the original key of A, substitute the **Amaj7** (sometimes written without the **j**) for the ordinary **A** major, and use the **Dmaj7** instead of the **D** major chord. If you make these changes in the verse, but keep to the original chords for the chorus, the whole song will sound much more interesting. Don't be put off

using these major seventh chords because they're more difficult to sing along to – it becomes much easier with practice.

Moveable Chord Shapes

Small Barres

When you finger the **F** chord, your first finger is doing what is known as a 'grand barre', or in other words a large or full barre across all the strings. Any barre over just some of the strings is known as a half barre, or a small barre. Both types are very important, particularly when playing further up the fretboard (or fingerboard). So let's take a look at two small-barre chords ...

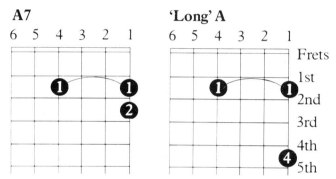

A7   'Long' A

Drop your left-hand thumb a little, and grip hard behind the first finger.

This is a little more difficult to keep the pressure on, but as always, with practice it becomes easier.

Chord shapes can move up the fretboard, and change name in the same way as individual notes. So if you do the same shape as the **A7** above, moved up just two frets, it becomes a **B7**! Try it. Now move that same shape one more fret toward the body of the guitar and what does it become? Yes, a **C7**. The one **drawback** to this moveable shape routine is that the **open strings** used at the start (when the shape is an **A7**), i.e. the open 5th and 6th strings in this case, **often cannot be used** when the shape is further up the neck. So to start with, play only the strings that are being pressed down with the left hand – all these strings will have changed by the same number of frets, so they'll all be part of the new chord.

Large Barres

I've already given you three chords that use the full barre across the six strings – the **F**, **F♯m**, and **Bm** chords. These shapes aren't particularly easy to start with, but they're extremely useful for getting variety into your playing. Also, when you can do just a few of them, you really know many more chords – by using the same shape up the fretboard, you can produce another ten chords! Let's take a look at the **E** chord first, and see the other chords that can be produced by moving the same shape further up . . .

Now let's do the same sort of thing with the **E** minor chord – you know the **F♯** minor barre chord that comes from the **Em** chord already . . .

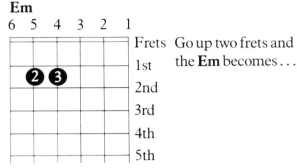

Em

Frets: Go up two frets and the **Em** becomes . . .

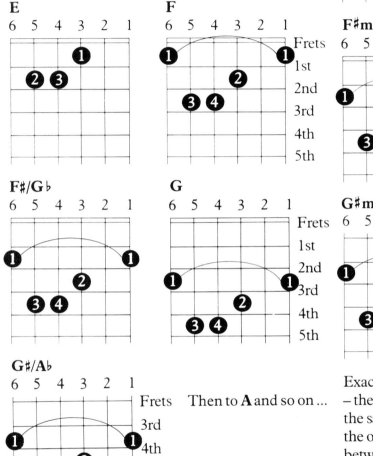

E

F

F♯/G♭

G

G♯/A♭

Then to **A** and so on . . .

Look at the **E** chord. Now examine the shape formed by the second, third, and fourth fingers in the **F** chord – see any similarity? So the notes on the 3rd, 4th, and 5th strings have gone up by one fret or semitone, but what about the 6th, 2nd, and 1st strings that are played open in an **E** chord? Well, the barre with the first finger takes care of them. When you play an **F**, therefore, you're really playing that familiar **E** chord shape, one fret up. Write down the next few chords produced by moving this shape up the neck.

F♯m

Gm

G♯m/A♭m

Am

Exactly the same thing happens with the **Em** shape – the barre takes what were the open strings up by the same number of frets as the other fingers doing the original **Em** shape. I've missed one chord between **Em** and **F♯m** – what is it? Can you also find the next few chords further up the neck?

And now the **Am** chord . . .

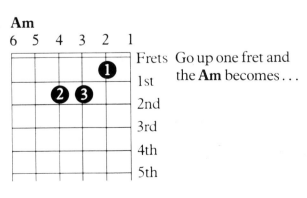

Am

Frets: Go up one fret and the **Am** becomes . . .

7

Large Barres Continued

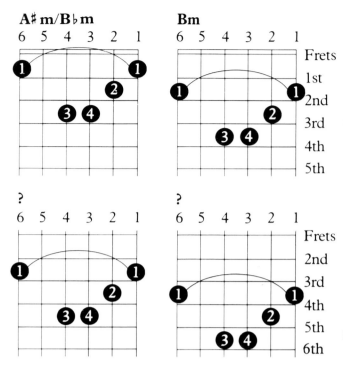

A♯m/B♭m

Bm

?

?

I'd like you to fill in the two missing chord names above, and also find the next few chords further up the neck like before. This is a very useful exercise, because there are hundreds of chords produced up the fretboard by shapes you already know!

string additions, but without the necessity of missing out the 5th string. Let's have a look at these possibilities . . .

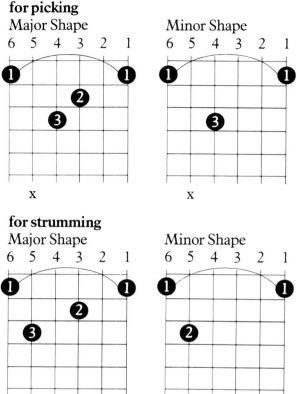

for picking

Major Shape

Minor Shape

for strumming

Major Shape

Minor Shape

Other Large Barres

Many of the chord shapes you've been using so far can be taken up the fretboard with the barre. Some, however, are much more difficult to finger than the three shown above, so for the moment we won't look at those. But the **Emaj7**, the **Amaj7**, the **Em7**, the **Am7**, the **E7**, and the **A7** can all produce other chords up the neck in exactly the same way as those above – see if you can write out and play the barre chords that come from these six chords (See the **F7** chord on page 5 for the **E7** shape that you use).

In order to free the little finger for adding passing notes or hammer-ons, the barre-chord shape may be amended. One standard thing to do when playing a barre **F** minor or **F** major shape, is to move the third finger to the 4th string, and the little finger is then available to add notes on the treble strings. This is suitable for picking in particular, because the thumb strikes are generally on the 6th and 4th strings – the 5th string is not played in this position. When strumming, the seventh position can be used, and the fourth finger is again available for treble-

Twelve-Bar Blues In **G**

The twelve-bar blues sequence is a very useful one for experimenting with new chord shapes or positions on the fretboard, so let's try substituting some of the new chord positions for the normal ones . . .

4/4 Swing

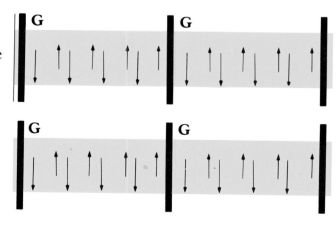

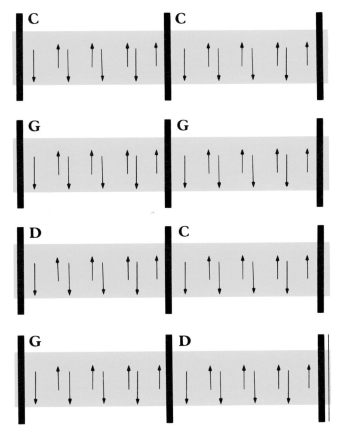

The sequence above is in its most elementary form – no **seventh** chords are shown at all. Play it through using the normal chord positions first. Right, that should be the same as you played it when you transposed the original blues sequence I gave you to the key of G (without the **seventh** chords). Now I want you to go through these steps:

Find out and remember where the **E** shape (or, if you like, the **F** shape) becomes a **G** chord, a **C** chord, and a **D** chord. Now use these positions for the blues sequence above.

Now have a look at the **G7, C7,** and **D7** alternative chord shapes below. . .

E7 Shape

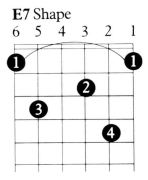

This shape becomes an **F7** on the 1st fret (as shown), and a **G7** on the 3rd fret. Try using this shape in the fourth and eighth bars. If you want a

"heavier" sounding seventh chord, use the little finger as shown – try both types anyway.

A7 Shape

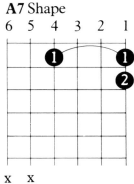

This shape is a **G♯7** or **A♭7** when used on the 1st fret. On the 2nd fret it's an **A7**, as shown previously, and with the barre on the 5th fret it becomes a **C7**. Move the same shape two more frets further up and it becomes a **D7**. So try using this type of **C7** for the fifth, sixth, and tenth bars. And the **D7** for the ninth and twelfth bars.

Once you're used to the G blues sequence and these new small and large barres, try using them when playing in the other keys. In the key of E for example, the **E** (or **F** shape) on the 5th fret is an **A**, and on the 7th fret is a **B**.

Whenever you're playing the songs you've learned, think about the possibility of using the same chords in different positions – perhaps just for the chorus, or the middle section, if there is one.

Barre chords are extremely important in the rock guitar area, but many folk players use them too – a technique called 'damping' requires barre chords, and most players in all modern types of music use them. So practice fingering them and don't worry if every note isn't crystal clear every time – gradually your fingers and hand become stronger, and your technique improves. When you feel your hand getting tired, play some nonbarre chords, and come back to them when you're ready – take it a bit at a time, as long as it's regular practice.

Chords

9

And I Love Her · Lennon/McCartney

Chords (side margin)

Here's a beautiful song from the Beatles, arranged in the key of E. Two of the chords must be played with a barre, the **F♯m** and **C♯m**. You could use the usual positions for the **A** and **B** chords, but I'd like you to use the **F** shape on the 5th and 7th frets for those – then your left hand can rest when it comes back to the **E**.

Accompaniment 4/4 Rhythm   ↓↑ = Strum down/up

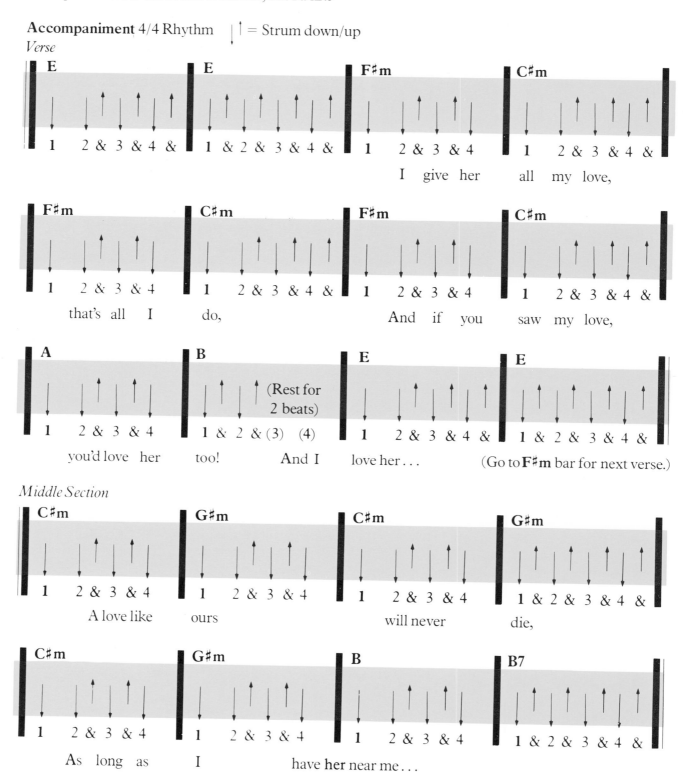

Verse

Middle Section

Notes
Practice moving from one barre chord to another, before trying the whole song. The **G♯m** chord involves the same shape as the **F♯m**, just two frets up. For the **B7** chord, use one of the shapes I've shown you, with a barre on the 7th fret.

Mellow Yellow Donovan

Damping means stopping the strings ringing after you've hit them with the right hand (or plectrum). It's an extremely important technique in rock music, but comes into jazz, modern and traditional folk, and blues music.

The bigger the barre, the better the damping effect will be, because the left hand can stop more strings ringing. Finger an **F** chord. Now hit all the strings with your right hand, i.e. a quick strum. Then, just as the strings start to ring, ease off the pressure of your left hand, but keep touching the strings – in

that way you'll damp the sound.

In the arrangement below, you've got just two full barre chords – the **G** and **A**. Both of these are the **F** shape moved up. I hope you can work out what fret they're on. The key chord, **D**, could also be a barre but I want you to play the ordinary one for the moment (to give your hand a rest every now and again!) – concentrate on hitting the top three treble strings with the right hand though, and then the damping on those strings with the left hand will be more effective.

Accompaniment 4/4 Swing Rhythm ↓↑ = Strum down/up (all downstrokes should be damped)

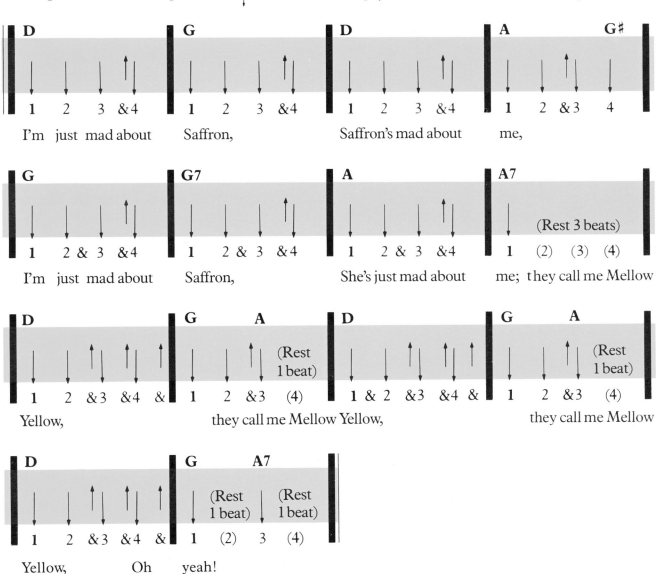

Notes
Where I've shown **G7** and **A7**, use one of the barre versions that you know.
The chord run from **A** down to **G** involves a **G♯**.

Use the same **F** shape, barre 4th fret. Damp **all** downstrokes **except** those just before a rest.
Try to get a nice bounce into this accompaniment!

11

Tablature Explained

When starting to play the guitar, it's enough to have to master the physical side of learning – so you were given accompaniments in what may be called 'simple notation'. For the strumming and bass-strum techniques this type of notation saves a huge amount of individual note-writing, and for the arpeggio and alternating thumb techniques it is adequate for the straightforward patterns. But for more advanced playing the simple notation cannot be used – so either you can read and write your complicated arrangements in ordinary musical notation (which I've given you mainly for the classical pieces), or you can use 'tablature' . . .

What Is Tablature?

Tablature is a kind of pictorial method of notation, and uses six lines going across – these lines represent the six strings of the guitar. It was in use hundreds of years ago, for writing down lute music. Though it doesn't show quite as much detail as ordinary musical notation, it does show every note that is played. Apart from these facts, for anybody who's interested in blues and modern picking styles, a great deal of material is now published which uses tablature – including my three books in the *Folk Guitar Styles of Today* series.

Tablature Explained

As I said above, tablature uses six lines going across the page, and these lines represent the six strings of the guitar. The top line is the 1st string, i.e. the thinnest, and the bottom is the bass 6th string. Let's take a look at a sample bar of music written in tablature . . .

The chord for the bar is shown as normal above the notation. So finger an ordinary **G** chord to begin with. Now working from left to right, this is what you'd do . . .

Play the 6th string, 3rd fret with your right hand thumb, together with the 1st string, 3rd fret. **You must decide** whether to use your index, middle or ring right-hand finger for this. I'm sure you recognize that this is a 'pinch'. **If two notes are vertically in line, they must be played at the same time.**

Now the thumb plays the open 4th string on the second beat, followed by a right-hand finger playing the open 2nd string. So far you've counted 1, 2& . . .

The thumb plays the third beat note: 6th string, 3rd fret again, followed by the 1st string, 3rd fret again, and finally the last beat is the thumb playing the open 4th string again. So the whole bar is counted: 1, 2&, 3&, 4.

You may have recognized that bar by now as being an alternating thumb pattern that you learned a while ago. If we played only patterns like that, there would be no need to use tablature but because we want to advance a bit, it's necessary – random notes will be coming in, and more treble strings will be involved.

So the tablature tells you the rhythm, where the beats are, where the thumb-strikes are, what fret your left-hand fingers must press down, and the chord is shown above each bar. You must decide which fingers on your right and left hands to use, and to count each bar carefully before trying it.

Tablature Samples

Notation Comparison

To make sure you understand tablature, have a look at two familiar patterns, one from the arpeggio style and the other alternating thumb, both written out in 'simple' notation, tablature, and finally standard music notation...

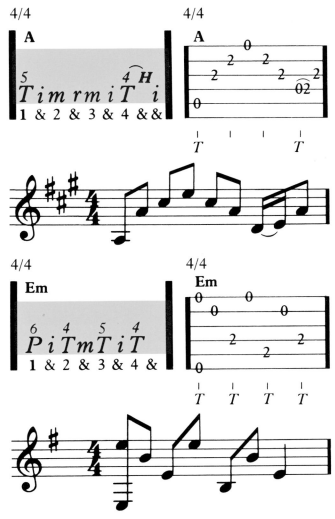

Bass Runs

Most of what you've learned so far, like the patterns above, doesn't involve a great deal of coordination between the left and right hands. But occasionally you did have to move your left-hand fingers away from their "usual" positions – for hammer-ons, bass runs, and (particularly in the classical pieces) treble passing notes. A hammer-on is shown easily in tablature (see above), and bass runs also...

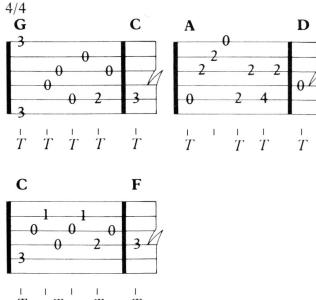

Passing Notes

In the classical pieces you had passing notes, with the left-hand fingers having to move away from their usual places. In some of the accompaniments that follow, passing notes and notes played in different places on the fretboard will be shown in tablature – the simple notation would be overloaded with these variations. Try a few sample bars containing some of the ideas that will follow...

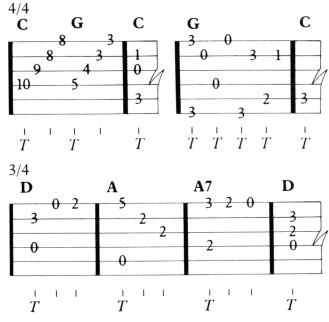

Streets Of London Ralph McTell

Although the arrangement of "Streets Of London" in Book 3 sounded pretty good, by following the melody a little you can get a really interesting sound. Here's an introduction for the song, and you can steal some of the ideas in it for the accompaniment itself...

Introduction 4/4 Rhythm Tablature (see pages 12 and 13)

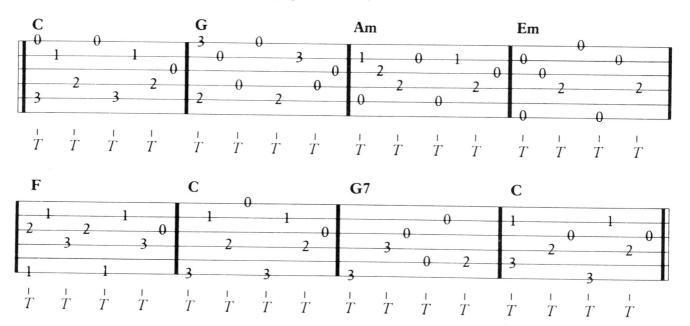

Notes

Count each bar carefully first. Then experiment with the fingering. Once you've got the rhythm and fingering straight in your mind, try the bar at a very slow speed.

The basic chord of the bar is shown above the tablature, but many notes mean changing your fingers around. Try using your second and fourth fingers in the 2nd bar, for instance, and then move your fourth from the 1st string to the 2nd string. Watch out for the last half-beat notes at the end of bars – often they're anticipating the chord change, and mean that you can be changing over chords at that point instead of the start of the next bar.

In bars six and eight, the **C** chord has a **G** bass note on the 6th string – use your third finger in both cases. In the seventh bar, the **G7** chord has its seventh on the 3rd fret, 4th string – use your fourth finger.

When you can get through all eight bars satisfactorily, take the tempo up a little. Then try putting some of these ideas into the song accompaniment itself.

Freight Train James and Williams

Here's another arrangement in the key of **C** – although Ralph McTell actually plays in the key of **E♭**, because he puts his capo on the 3rd fret – and here too the melody is picked out on the treble strings. The little finger comes in handy for a lot of this kind of picking, and yours will become stronger in time!

Like last time, go over each bar carefully, count it slowly, and try to keep the rhythm steady. That's very important. Then speed the whole accompaniment up when you can get through it without stopping.

Accompaniment 4/4 Rhythm Tablature (see pages 12 and 13)

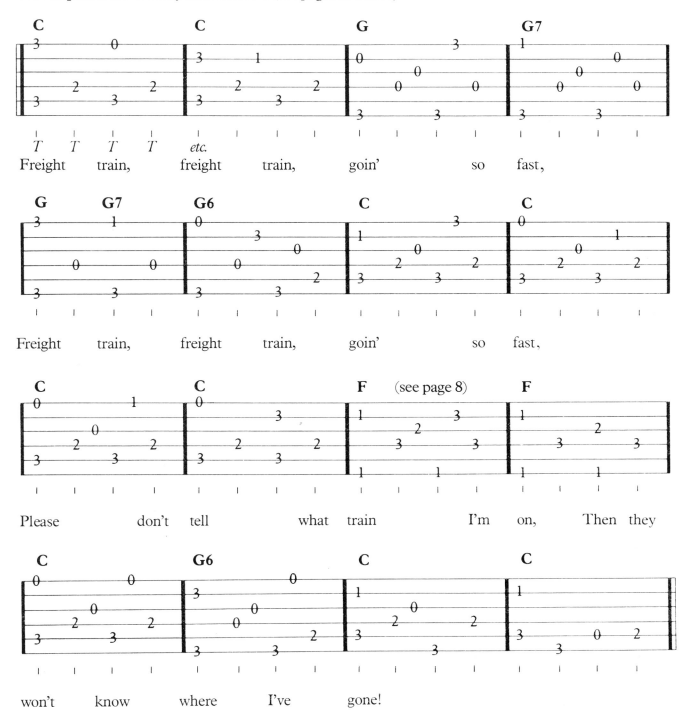

Freight train, freight train, goin' so fast,

Freight train, freight train, goin' so fast,

Please don't tell what train I'm on, Then they

won't know where I've gone!

Notes
The thumb of the right hand must play **all** the bass notes on the beat – I've shown the thumb indications only under the 1st bar.

As for the "Streets Of London" introduction, use your index finger on the right hand for those notes on the 3rd string. If you want to get some practice for fancy fingerpicking in the future, use your ring finger for the notes on the 1st string, and middle finger for those on the 2nd string. You can get by using just the index and middle fingers, however,

with many folk arrangements. **G6** is shown above two bars – a **G6** can be the same as a **G** major chord, but with no finger on the top string, i.e. with an **E** note added. In this case, the little finger moves to the 2nd string, 3rd fret for another **D** note.

No arrangement is sacred – try some changes if you want. For instance, put a bar of **E**, and a bar of **E7** instead of **C** in the ninth and tenth bars.

By cutting out some of the notes between the beats, the tempo can be increased more easily – that's why this song can be played faster than the last!

The Hammer-On

Some More Ideas

I used the word 'embellishments' to mean any technique that took us away from the patterns with which we started the various styles. One of these techniques was the hammer-on. So far you've used the hammer-on in one particular way – **off** the beat. That's to say the right hand has struck an open string **on** the beat, and the left-hand finger has come down to produce another note on the offbeat, or between beats. Let's have another look at the hammer-on you're familiar with...

Singly (on its own)   **Combined** (with bass)

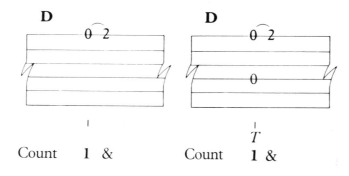

Count   **1**   &   Count   **1**   &

The hammer-on in both cases comes **between beats**. Though this is the most common timing, it's very useful to know how to do the hammer-on **on the beat:**

4/4 Arpeggio (Straight or Swing)

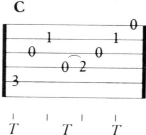

T   T   T
1 & 2 & 3 & 4 &

4/4 Alternating Thumb (Straight or Swing)

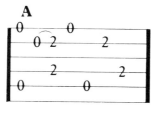

T   T   T   T
1 & 2 & 3 & 4

The first example above is quite easy, but follow these steps for the second one... Pinch the open 1st string together with the open 5th; then play the open 2nd string. That's '1&'. Now your left-hand finger comes down onto the 2nd string, 2nd fret. As it does so, your right-hand thumb must play the 4th string, 2nd fret. Thus the right hand strikes the bass at **exactly the same time** as the left hand hammers-on. And that's why the two notes are shown in a vertical line, even though they're not pinched together.

Have a go at a bar of **E** that includes both types of hammer-on...

4/4 Alternating Thumb

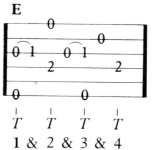

T   T   T   T
1 & 2 & 3 & 4

Try this bar with the swing rhythm first, then straight. You'll see that combining both types of hammer-on timing produces a very full sound.

Hammer-ons can also be produced in the strumming style – try doing one on the top string of a **D** chord like this...

And now hammer-on a whole **E** chord like this...

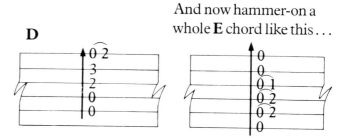

The same thing applies to the strum part of the bass-strum style. Strumming can sound boring sometimes, so you should try to use some embellishments to brighten it up a bit. You'll find yourself doing hammer-ons in all styles after you've been playing awhile.

Sunday Blues Russ Shipton

The Monotonic Bass Style

Though it's got a long name, this style is quite easy to understand and to play. Monotonic just means that the bass notes stay the same for each chord, instead of changing back and forth like the alternating thumb style, for instance.

As well as illustrating this new style, the twelve-bar blues sequence in **E** below also shows you how to use hammer-ons both on and off the beat. Toward the end, you'll find hammer-ons that involve a fretted first note – in other words, the hammer-on goes from one left-hand finger to another, instead of from an open string to a left-hand finger. Try these three examples first . . .

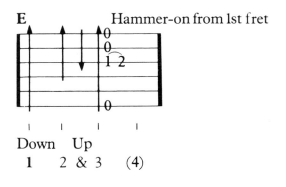

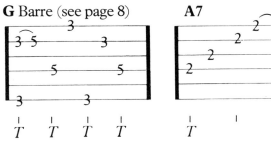

Instrumental 4/4 Swing or Straight Rhythm

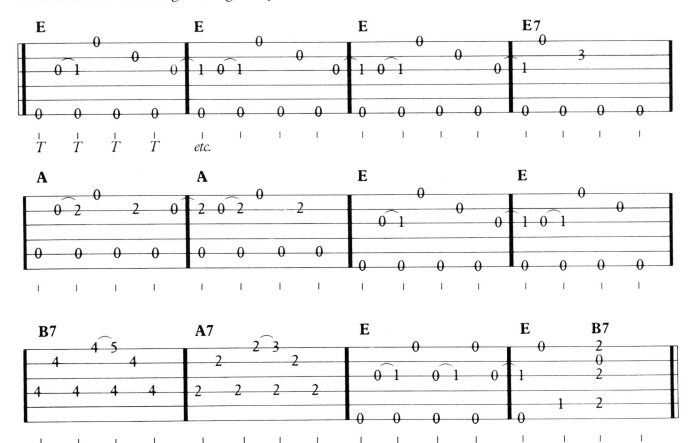

Notes

Try the swing rhythm first, and take it slow and steady. The pulsing monotonic bass has to be firm and regular. All the hammer-ons are **on** to the beat, except one in the eleventh bar.

The **B7** and **A7** are the half barre, or small barre shapes (though not the final **B7** which is the usual position – hold that one for two beats).

17

The Pull-Off

Pull-offs are the opposite of hammer-ons. Normally they involve the right hand playing a string that is pressed down by the left hand, usually on the 1st or 2nd fret, and the left-hand finger coming off the string to produce another note, the note of the open string. 'Pull' is used, because the left-hand finger needs to pull the string slightly before releasing it, in order to produce a loud enough note. Let's try a pull-off, first without a bass, and then with . . .

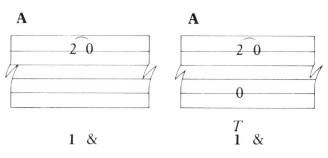

And now, onto the beat . . .

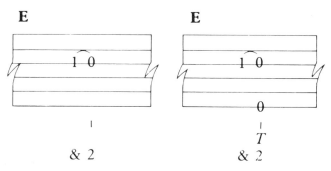

Try doing a few more, using the chords you know at the bottom of the fretboard. Now have a look at pull-offs that don't finish with an open string . . .

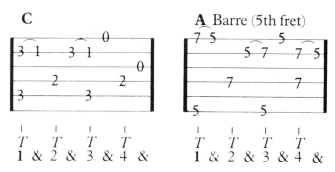

Now you can do the same thing with pull-offs as you can with hammer-ons. Let's see if we can combine hammer-ons and pull-offs – it's very effective when you can do it.

4/4 Arpeggio

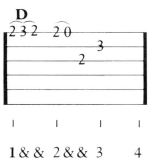

4/4 Alternating Thumb

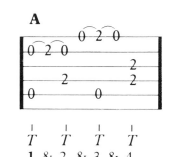

So your right hand strikes just once to produce two further notes from the left hand. You can get even more, but it takes a while to strengthen the left hand enough. Experiment to see how many clear notes you can produce with your left hand, after your right hand has struck.

Down By The Brook · Russ Shipton

Here's a short instrumental to give you some
practice at doing pull-offs. Remember to pull the
string a bit before releasing it . . .

Instrumental 4/4 Rhythm

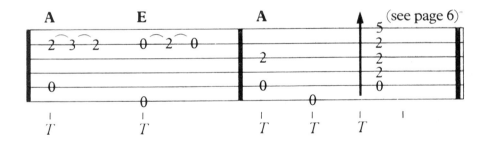

Notes

Just before the fourth bar you change to an **E** chord –
gradually. Your first finger goes down for the
hammer-on to start, then your second and third
fingers on the 4th and 5th strings. Finally, your
fourth finger goes on for the **D** note.
Pause for one beat at the end of both the sixth and
eighth bars. Play a 'long **A**' in the last bar (from the
first beat), and let it ring on for that last beat.
You can use your first and second fingers for the first
hammer-on and pull-off in the seventh bar, and then
your first finger for the other one.
Count each bar carefully before playing it.

Slides, Bends, and Harmonics

Slides

Slides are generally used by the advanced players, but like everything else, in time you'll get accurate with these embellishments too. What a slide is must be pretty obvious from the name. Open strings don't come into this operation, because you slide from one fret to a higher fret, or a lower fret. Naturally this is done on the same string, but many players, particularly blues guitarists, slide several notes at the same time. Let's have a look at slides in the same way as we examined hammer-ons and pull-offs:

/= Slide (Use your first finger to begin with)

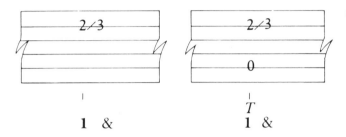

1 &   **1 &**

And now, on the beat . . .

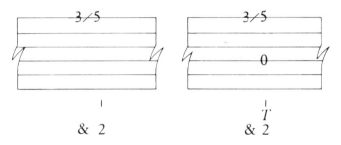

& 2   **& 2**

Now try similar slides on and off the beat, but going from a higher to a lower fret. Once you're happy with that, have a go at sliding more than one note at a time. Try to get nice clear notes. . .

Use first and second fingers.

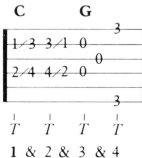

1 & 2 & 3 & 4

Use full chord shapes.

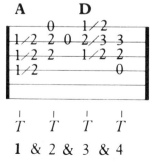

1 & 2 & 3 & 4

Bends

'Bend' means to stretch a string. Sometimes lead players will bend a string to produce a note a full tone higher than the fret their finger is on, but they are using very light strings, and need to bend strings a lot to get the effect they need. In most acoustic playing, just a half tone or less is sufficient. The sign for a bend is usually a small arrow, placed just to the right of the note . . .

And now with a bass . . .

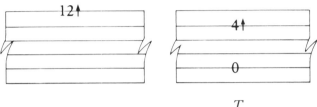

Play the note with your right hand and then push the string upward (or pull downward if you prefer) to create a higher note.

There's a piece later in this section that has some bends in it, so once you've got the hang of stretching the strings (usually the treble) have a go at that.

Harmonics

A dot placed after the note means a 'harmonic' in tablature. Place your left-hand finger (any one) exactly over the fretwire that comes after the fret shown, and just touch it without pressing it onto the neck. Then strike the string with a flatpick or your thumb and remove the left-hand finger very quickly. After a bit of practice, you should produce a bell-like tone. Try doing them on the 12th (the easiest), 5th, and 7th frets.

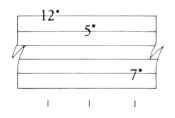

Skateboarding In The Park Russ Shipton

Here's a piece for practicing your slides, but it does have a few other ideas in it. It's essentially an arpeggio style that's involved, but your right-hand thumb is doing a bit more than usual – watch out for the thumb indications. In this instrumental, the slides are done by the left-hand second finger. That means you should use the fingering of **G** which has the third finger on the 6th string and second finger on the 5th.

Apart from the last slide, the second finger does the slide, and then comes back to the position it started from.

Instrumental 3/4 Rhythm

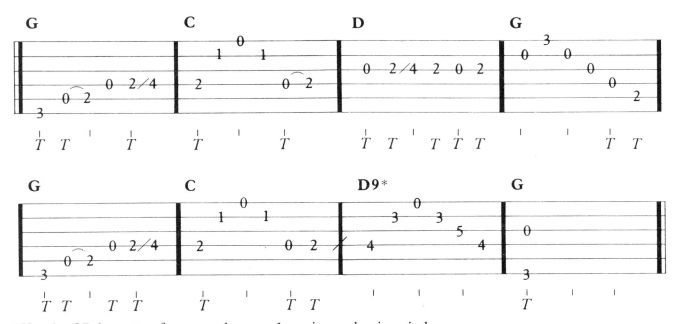

*Use the **C7** shape, two frets up – the open 1st string makes it a ninth.

Little Ben (Clock Chime) Russ Shipton

Instrumental 5/4 Rhythm

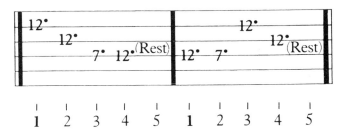

Don't worry about the 5/4 rhythm, it's pretty obvious how to play it. The pause could be longer than a beat, but it's interesting to know what 5/4 rhythm sounds like. Listen to Dave Brubeck's "Take Five," and you'll see that it can work very well!

You can also use harmonics to help you tune your guitar. The one on the 7th fret, 5th string is an **E** note, and can be checked with the open 1st string. And the harmonic on the 7th fret, 6th string is a **B** note and can be checked with the open 2nd string. You can easily make mistakes going from 1st to 6th string in tuning, so harmonics are a useful check.

Watermelon Russ Shipton

D-Bass Tuning

This piece has the most common variation to standard tuning; classical and modern guitarists make use of this one, and all you have to do is tune

the 6th string down by one tone – test it against your 4th string, it should be one octave below. Tuning the bottom string down to **D** gives a lot more flexibility to the left hand for moving around the fretboard, while the right hand hits the open bass strings.

Instrumental 4/4 Rhythm D-bass tuning

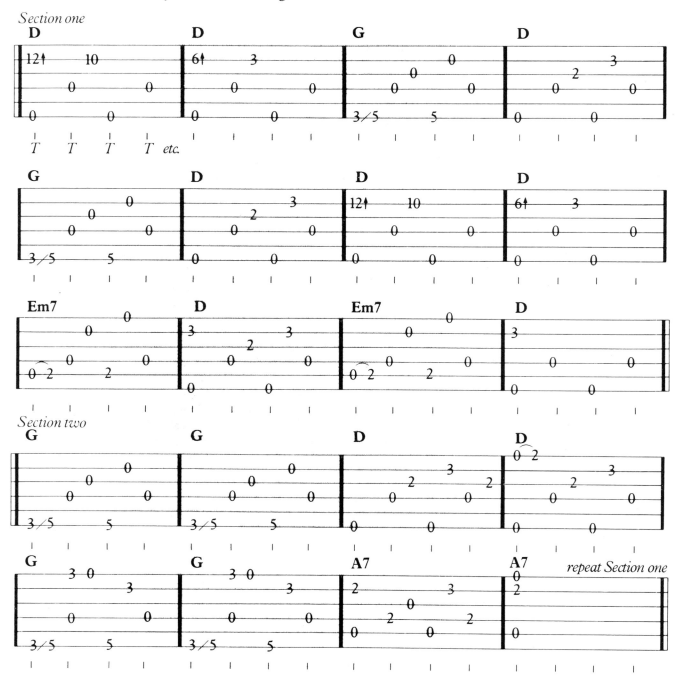

Notes

As usual, take each bar separately, count it and play it slowly. Then when you can remember the piece well enough to put it all together, try to take it a bit faster. Eventually, this instrumental should be played quite fast.

One way of fingering the first bar is with the third and first fingers. Then you could try your fourth finger for the next wow on the first beat of the second bar. The rest of the fingering is quite straightforward. Keep those bass notes nice and steady.

If You Could Read My Mind   Gordon Lightfoot

This melody has a lilt to it, so I've chosen a combination of syncopated arpeggio and alternating thumb patterns to use for an accompaniment. The thumb plays the first two notes of most bars.

Quite a few different chords come into this arrangement. The **G9** involves adding the **A** note to a **G** chord. The **Gsus** means adding a **C** note to the **G** chord. **Am7** is not the one you've played before – this one has two seventh notes.

Accompaniment 4/4 Rhythm

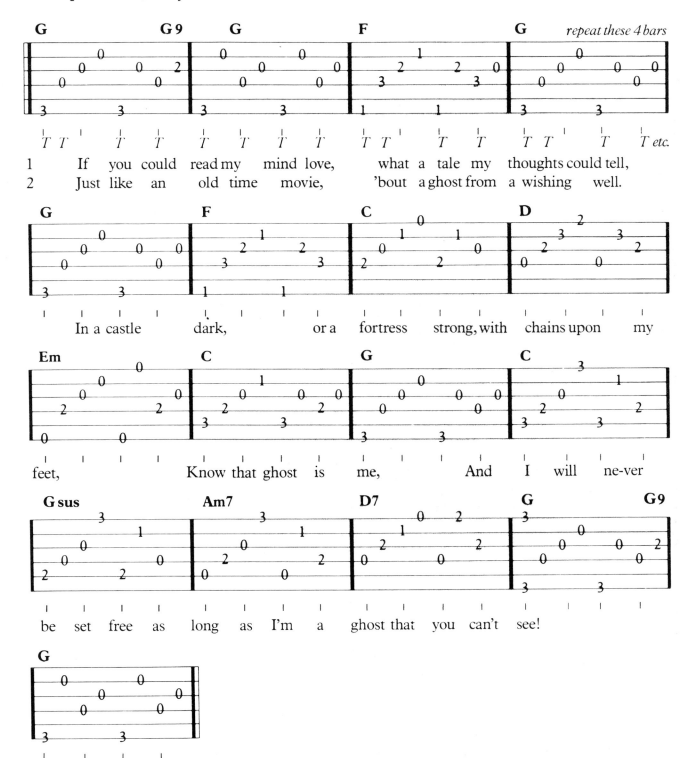

23

Useful Information

Eighth-Note Triplet

You've seen eighth notes singly and in groups, and in all cases they each amount in time value to one-half of a quarter note. But **sometimes** eighth notes are shown in groups of three – this is when a small 3 is put over the group to indicate a **triplet**. Each eighth note has the same time value as the others, but they all add up to just **one quarter note** . . .

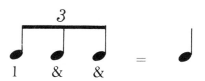

You've also learned that when a dot is placed after a note, it increases its time value by half again. So a dotted eighth note will last for one and one-half eighth-notes, in other words three sixteenth-notes. Very often, however, there is another note following the dotted eighth note that has its time value reduced accordingly by the same amount, i.e. to a sixteenth note . . .

Finger Signs

So far we have used *i*, *m*, *r*, and *T* for the right-hand signs. In fact, music in the classical idiom usually has these letters to indicate fingers and thumb . . .
i = index finger   *m* = middle finger   *a* = third or ring finger   *p* = thumb

Mid-Bar Start

All the pieces you've had so far begin at the start of a bar. In many cases there is a lead-in of a note or two, which is an essential part of the melody. No rest signs need be used for the split bar at the beginning, because the bar at the end of the section is correspondingly short in time value. This will be clearer when you come to the pieces that involve this writing device.

Different Ways Of Writing

Not everybody notates their music in exactly the same way, though most conventions are followed similarly. In one of the pieces that are coming up, for ease of writing, rest signs aren't used for the treble part, instead some of the bass notes are deemed to be both bass and treble. This is just one example of possible changes, but be on the look out for different notation styles.

The Bass Clef

Though I'm not going to use the bass clef in this course, it would be extremely useful for you to know at least enough about it to work out what notes are where. 'Clef' means the particular area of notes being considered, and so far you've been using just the treble clef, which involves the higher notes. The bass clef is the group of staff lines below the treble clef, on which are shown the lower notes. lower notes.

When the pianist-arrangers write out the music of a song, or a piece of classical music, the melody line is usually on a separate staff at the top, and the treble clef is used. Another staff, again the treble clef being used, shows the treble part (which often includes most of the melody). Finally, at the bottom, is the bass clef staff – this shows the bass part (bass runs, notes harmonizing with the melody, etc.). For the pianist, the treble part is played with his right hand, and the bass part with his left hand. Let's have a look at the notes in the bass clef . . .

This is the old sign for **f**. It signifies the bass clef/staff.

Air In C Fernando Sor

Fernando Sor wrote many small pieces and studies for learners of the guitar, and this is a simple but melodic one.

Use your first two fingers of the left hand for the **C** and **E** notes of the **C** chord, and then your third and fourth fingers for the **D** and **F** notes that follow soon after. For the right hand, there are pinches involving the thumb and middle finger, and the notes in between (usually the open 3rd string **G** note) would be played by the index finger. The more unusual bars have some fingering shown (the left-hand next to the note and the right-hand above).

When you've got the piece under control and memorized, try to play it quite fast . . .

Instrumental 4/4 Rhythm Standard music notation

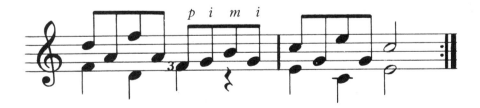

Greensleeves   Traditional, arranged Russ Shipton

This wonderful song from hundreds of years ago gives me a chance to give you something in the 3/8 rhythm. So far you've seen 4/4, 3/4, and 2/4 rhythms written in standard music notation, but none with an '8' on the bottom. That means each beat (three per bar, according to the top number) lasts for just one eighth note, which is half a quarter note. Many waltzes are written in this timing.

Instrumental 3/8 Rhythm Standard music notation

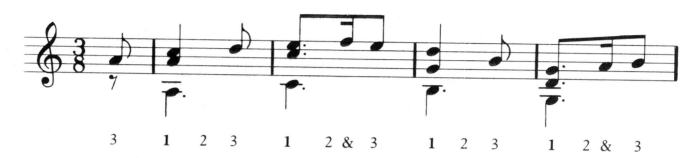

Notes

This piece is in A minor – try to work out the chords, after you've discovered the fingering. It's all on the first three frets, except the third bar from the end – use your little finger on the 4th fret, 4th string for the **F sharp** note. **Notice** also that the sharp sign for the **G** note in that bar applies to the other **G** note in the bar as well!

Those bars that have the dotted eighth note are a bit tricky – delay the dotted eighth note for two counts, and then the sixteenth note comes in on the offbeat.

26

Study Fernando Sor

This flowing, gentle study by Fernando Sor will give you valuable practice in bass and treble combinations – sometimes holding the bass, at other times holding the treble. Also there are pull-offs and bass and treble combined runs.

Instrumental 4/4 Rhythm sometimes shown as C Standard music notation

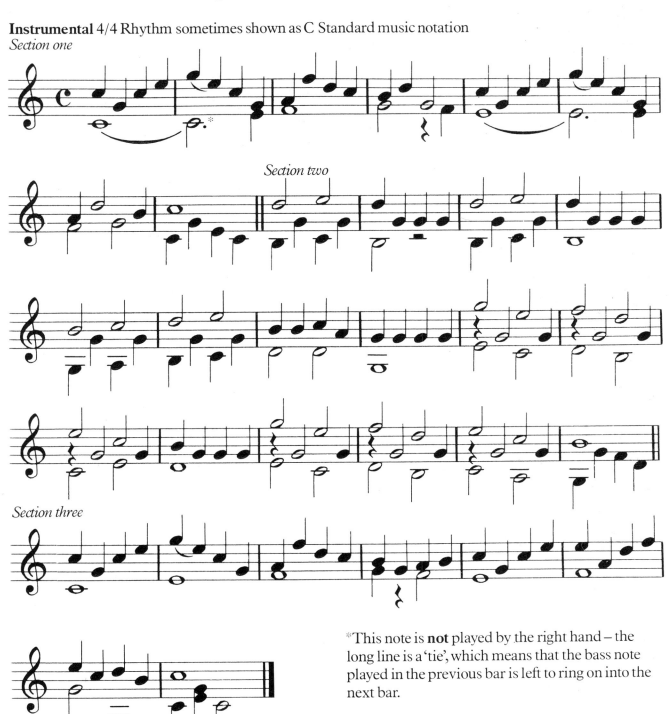

Section one

Section two

Section three

*This note is **not** played by the right hand – the long line is a 'tie', which means that the bass note played in the previous bar is left to ring on into the next bar.

Notes
I've split this study into three sections – take each section at a time, and then it'll be easier to handle the whole piece. The fingering is quite straightforward, and all on the first three frets. But the timing in bars nine, ten and eleven, and thirteen, fourteen and fifteen of the second section may look a bit odd. That's because a third part is shown. So you have the treble part on top, the middle part below that, and the bass at the bottom – all three must "add up" to a time value of four quarter-notes each.

Study   Matteo Carcassi

Here is part of a study that will eventually be played fast, once you've mastered the fingering and remembered the sequence. Four sixteenth-notes are used for every beat, each of them having an equal time value. Some fingering indications have been given. Try to make the bass notes ring out . . .

Instrumental 4/4 Rhythm

1 & & & 2 & & & 3 & & & 4 & & & *etc.*

Note
The bass notes are written as part of the treble (as sixteenth notes) **and** as part of the bass (as quarter notes).

Dance   Traditional, arranged Russ Shipton

This well-known tune is written in 6/8 time, which means there are six beats per bar, and each beat lasts for one eighth-note. Count each bar carefully, and you shouldn't have too much difficulty coping with this rhythm.

You'll see that this piece starts on the fifth beat of a bar, and the last bar of each section shows no rest signs – this is the usual convention.

The chords involved are mainly **A** and **E**, until the second section, when a full bar of **D** is used. Try to use only those fingers that are necessary, though.

This piece should be lively, and eventually played quite fast.

Instrumental 6/8 Rhythm Standard music notation

Section one

5 6   **1** 2 3 4 5 6   **1** 2 3 4 5 6   *etc.*

Section two

Note
Play the first section, repeat it (the dots send you back to the start). Then go on to the second section, and repeat that section too (the dots there send you back to the reverse-facing dots).

Romanza   Traditional, arranged Russ Shipton

This is perhaps the best known classical piece of all. A very romantic, gentle sound, as the title suggests. Though you have to explore the upper reaches of the fingerboard, things don't get complicated or difficult until you reach the seventh bar.

Here you have to do a half or small barre (as shown on the next page – this was also examined on page 6 of this book). Then you have to do a full barre for the **B** chord. That is also shown at the foot of the next page.

Instrumental 3/4 Rhythm Standard music notation   (Each group of three eighth-notes is a triplet=one beat)

1   &   &   2   &   &   3   &   &   *etc.*

Note
The **left**-hand fingering is shown above the notation. The right-hand fingering is straightforward – ring finger and bass together,

followed by the middle finger, and then the index finger. This pattern is repeated over and over again.

Romanza Continued

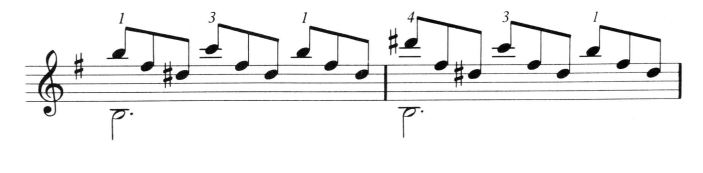

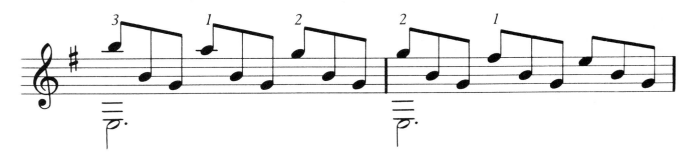

Chord Fingerings

In the seventh and eighth bars on the previous page, a half barre must be employed. This is similar to the one shown on page 6 of this book but the barre need only cover three strings. The first finger stays down, while the little and third fingers hold their respective **C** and **B** notes.

Similarly, the full barre position for the **B** chord in the ninth and tenth bars above, is not quite the same as the **F** shape you're used to – because the 6th string only is providing the bass part, the third and fourth fingers can be hovering for use on the treble strings.

Unfortunately both the notes of the melody aren't easy to make clear while holding down the barre, but persevere!

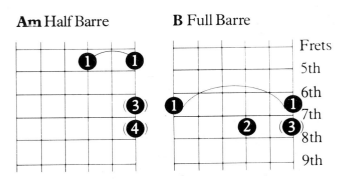

Am Half Barre   **B** Full Barre

Lyrics

And I Love Her

Verse 1:
I give her all my love, that's all I do,
And if you saw my love, you'd love her too,
And I love her . . .
Middle Section:
A love like ours will never die,
As long as I have her near me.
Verse 2:
She gives me everything, and tenderly
The kiss my lover brings, she brings to me
And I love her.
Verse 3:
Bright are the stars that shine, dark is the sky
I know this love of mine will never die
And I love her.

Mellow Yellow

Verse 1:
I'm just mad about Saffron, Saffron's mad about me,
I'm just mad about Saffron, she's just mad about me.
They call me mellow yellow, they call me mellow yellow,
They call me mellow yellow. Oh yeah!
Verse 2:
I'm just mad about fourteen, fourteen's mad about me,
I'm just mad about fourteen, fourteen's mad about me.
They call me mellow yellow, they call me mellow yellow,
They call me mellow yellow.
Verse 3:
Born high forever to fly, wind velocity nil
Born high forever to fly, if you want your cup I will fill.
They call me mellow yellow, they call me mellow yellow,
They call me mellow yellow.
Verse 4:
Electrical banana, is gonna be a sudden craze,
Electrical banana, is bound to be the very next phase.
They call me mellow yellow, they call me mellow yellow,
They call me mellow yellow.

Freight Train

Verse/Chorus:
Freight train, freight train, goin' so fast.
Freight train, freight train, goin' so fast.
Please don't tell what train I'm on,
Then they won't know where I've gone.
Verse 2:
When I'm dead and in my grave
No more good times will I crave.
Place the stones at my head and feet
And tell them that I've gone to sleep.
Verse 3:
When I die, Lord, bury me deep,
Way down on old Chestnut Street,
So I can hear old number nine
As she comes rollin' by.
Verse 4:
When I die, Lord, bury me deep,
Way down on old Chestnut Street.
Place the stones at my head and feet
And tell them that I'm still asleep.

If You Could Read My Mind

Verse 1:
If you could read my mind love, what a tale my thoughts could tell,
Just like an old time movie, 'bout a ghost from a wishing well,
In a castle dark, or a fortress strong, with chains upon my feet,
Know that ghost is me, and I will never be set free,
As long as I'm a ghost that you can't see!
Verse 2:
If I could read your mind love, what a tale your thoughts could tell
Just like a paperback novel, the kind that drug stores sell.
Then you reached the part where the heartaches come, the hero would be me,
But heroes often fail, and you won't read that book again,
Because the ending's just too hard to take!
Middle Section:
I'd walk away, like a movie star who gets burned in a three-way script,
Enter number two: a movie queen to play the scene of bringing all the good things out of me.
But for now love, let's be real – I never thought I could feel this way
And I've got to say that I just don't get it. I don't know where we went wrong,
But the feeling's gone and I just can't get it back!
Verse 3:
If you could read my mind love, what a tale my thoughts could tell,
Just like an old time movie, 'bout a ghost from a wishing well,
In a castle dark, or a fortress strong, with chains upon my feet,
But stories always end, and if you read between the lines
You'd know that I'm just trying to understand the feelings that you lack.
I never thought I could feel this way and I've got to say that I just don't get it,
I don't know where we went wrong, but the feeling's gone and I just can't get it back!

Closing Comments

Well, you've made it to the end of the course, and by now you're a pretty competent player. To keep things moving, though, you'll need to listen to artists (in clubs and on record), learn from other books and publications, and at the same time experiment to develop your own distinctive sounds.

In order to give you some idea of where to start reading and listening, I've listed some books below that cover guitar playing in the various categories that exist today (though the dividing lines are sometimes a bit hazy), and many of the exponents of these styles. I'll leave it to you to decide which particular records to buy, but often the earlier records of artists contain numbers with vocal and guitar parts alone – listen to several albums and choose those that you think are most suitable for your development.

Many great songs aren't published in simple notation or tablature forms, but only in sheet music, using standard music notation. Now you're able to read the treble and bass clefs, you can pick up many valuable ideas for an accompaniment from the sheet music, even though the arrangement will be by a pianist, and for pianists.

Some of you may be interested only in playing the guitar to yourself or friends at home. Others may want to become semiprofessional or fully professional in music. I hope that both groups of you have enjoyed this course, and will continue to get a lot of fun and relaxation from playing the guitar.

Books

Folk Guitar Styles of Today – Beginners ⎱
Folk Guitar Styles of Today   ⎰ Russ
Folk Guitar Styles of Today – Book 2   ⎰ Shipton

Fingerpicking Styles for Guitar – Happy Traum

Note Reading and Music Theory for Folk Guitarists – Jerry Silverman

Rock Guitar – Happy and Artie Traum

Folksinger's Guide to the Classical Guitar – Harvey Vinson

Complete Course in Jazz Guitar – Mickey Baker (Lewis Music)

English Folk Guitar – Mike Raven (Stafford Guitar Centre)

(All published by Music Sales Ltd, except where otherwise stated. Music Sales also publish many tutors on blues and ragtime playing, and books of classical pieces or arrangements).

Players

American Folk/Pop
Don McLean
Paul Simon
Joni Mitchell (early)
Leonard Cohen
John Stewart
John Denver
Neil Young
Steve Stills
Tom Paxton
Bob Dylan
James Taylor
Arlo Guthrie

Jazz
Mickey Baker
Joe Pass
Barney Kessel
John McLaughlin

American Traditional
(Including Blues)
Happy Traum
Stefan Grossman
Rev. Gary Davis
Tom Rush
The Kingston Trio
Big Bill Broonzy
Mississippi John Hurt

English Folk/Pop/Ragtime
Ralph McTell
Donovan
Cat Stevens
Al Stewart
Richard Digance
John James
Michael Chapman
Steve Tilston
Rab Noakes
Wizz Jones

English Traditional
Martin Carthy
Nic Jones
Mike Raven
Vin Garbutt

Classical/Flamenco
Andrés Segovia
John Williams
John Mills
Julian Bream
Paco Pena
Manitas De Plata